Murad the Unlucky & Other Tales by Maria Edgeworth

Maria Edgeworth was born at Black Bourton, Oxfordshire on January 1st 1768. Her early years were with her mother's family in England. Sadly, her mother died when Maria was five.

Maria was educated at Mrs Lattafière's school in Derby in 1775. There she studied dancing, French and other subjects. Maria transferred to Mrs Devis's school in Upper Wimpole Street, London. Her father began to focus more attention on Maria in 1781 when she nearly lost her sight to an eye infection.

She returned home to Ireland at 14 and took charge of her younger siblings. She herself was home-tutored by her father in Irish economics and politics, science, literature and law. Despite her youth literature was in her blood. Maria also became her father's assistant in managing the family's large Edgeworthstown estate.

Maria first published 1795 with 'Letters for Literary Ladies'. That same year 'An Essay on the Noble Science of Self-Justification', written for a female audience, advised women on how to obtain better rights in general and specifically from their husbands.

'Practical Education' (1798) is a progressive work on education. Maria's ambition was to create an independent thinker who understands the consequences of his or her actions.

Her first novel, 'Castle Rackrent' was published anonymously in 1800 without her father's knowledge. It was an immediate success and firmly established Maria's appeal to the public.

Her father married four times and the last of these to Frances, a year younger and a confidante of Maria, who pushed them to travel more widely: London, Britain and Europe were all now visited.

The second series of 'Tales of Fashionable Life' (1812) did so well that she was now the most commercially successful novelist of her age.

She particularly worked hard to improve the living standards of the poor in Edgeworthstown and to provide schools for the local children of all and any denomination.

After a visit to see her relations Maria had severe chest pains and died suddenly of a heart attack in Edgeworthstown on 22nd May 1849. She was 81.

Index of Contents

INTRODUCTION

Maria Edgeworth came of a lively family which had settled in Ireland in the latter part of the sixteenth century. Her father at the age of five- and-twenty inherited the family estates at Edgeworthstown in 1769. He had snatched an early marriage, which did not prove happy. He had a little son, whom he was educating upon the principles set forth in Rousseau's "Emile," and a daughter Maria, who was born on the 1st of January, 1767. He was then living at Hare Hatch, near Maidenhead. In March, 1773, his first wife died after giving birth to a daughter named Anna. In July, 1773, he married again, Honora Sneyd, and went to live in Ireland, taking with him his daughter Maria, who was then about six years old. Two years afterwards she was sent from Ireland to a school at Derby. In April, 1780, her father's second wife died, and advised him upon her death-bed to marry her sister Elizabeth. He married his deceased wife's sister on the next following Christmas Day. Maria Edgeworth was in that year removed to a school in London, and her holidays were often spent with her father's friend Thomas Day, the author of "Sandford and Merton," an eccentric enthusiast who lived then at Anningsley, in Surrey.

Maria Edgeworth—always a little body—was conspicuous among her schoolfellows for quick wit, and was apt alike for study and invention. She was story-teller general to the community. In 1782, at the age of fifteen, she left school and went home with her father and his third wife, who then settled finally at Edgeworthstown.

At Edgeworthstown Richard Lovell Edgeworth now became active in the direct training of his children, in the improvement of his estate, and in schemes for the improvement of the country. His eldest daughter, Maria, showing skill with the pen, he made her more and more his companion and fellow-worker to good ends. She kept household accounts, had entrusted to her the whole education of a little brother, wrote stories on a slate and read them to the family, wiped them off when not approved, and copied them in ink if they proved popular with the home public. Miss Edgeworth's first printed book was a plea for the education of women, "Letters to Literary Ladies," published in 1795, when her age was eight- and-twenty. Next year, 1796, working with her father, she produced the first volume of the "Parent's Assistant." In November, 1797, when Miss Edgeworth's age was nearly thirty-one, her father, then aged fifty-three, lost his third wife, and he married a fourth in the following May. The fourth wife, at first objected to, was young enough to be a companion and friend, and between her and Maria Edgeworth a fast friendship came to be established. In the year of her father's fourth marriage Maria joined him in the production of two volumes on "Practical Education." Then followed books for children, including "Harry and Lucy," which had been begun by her father years before in partnership with his second wife, when Thomas Day began writing "Sandford and Merton," with the original intention that it should be worked in as a part of the whole scheme.

In the year 1800 Miss Edgeworth, thirty-three years old, began her independent career as a novelist with "Castle Rackrent;" and from that time on, work followed work in illustration of the power of a woman of genius to associate quick wit and quick feeling with sound sense and a good reason for speaking. Sir Walter Scott in his frank way declared that he received an impulse from Miss Edgeworth's example as a story-teller. In the general preface to his own final edition of the Waverley Novels he said that "Without being so presumptuous as to hope to emulate the rich humour, pathetic tenderness, and admirable tact, which pervade the works of my accomplished friend, I felt that something might be attempted for my own country of the same kind with that which Miss Edgeworth so fortunately achieved for Ireland—something which might introduce her natives to those of the sister kingdom in a more favourable light than they had been placed hitherto, and tend to procure sympathy for their virtues and indulgence for their foibles."

Of the three stories in this volume, who—"Murad the Unlucky" and "The Limerick Gloves"—first appeared in three volumes of "Popular Tales," which were first published in 1804, with a short introduction by Miss Edgeworth's father. "Madame de Fleury" was written a few years later.

H. M.

MURAD THE UNLUCKY

CHAPTER I

It is well known that the grand seignior amuses himself by going at night, in disguise, through streets of Constantinople; as the caliph Haroun Alraschid used formerly to do in Bagdad.

One moonlight night, accompanied by his grand vizier, he traversed several of the principal streets of the city without seeing anything remarkable. At length, as they were passing a rope-maker's, the sultan recollected the Arabian story of Cogia-Hassan Alhabal, the rope-maker, and his two friends, Saad and Saadi, who differed so much in their opinion concerning the influence of fortune over human affairs.

"What is your opinion on this subject?" said the grand seignior to his vizier.

"I am inclined, please your majesty," replied the vizier, "to think that success in the world depends more upon prudence than upon what is called luck, or fortune."

"And I," said the sultan, "am persuaded that fortune does more for men than prudence. Do you not every day hear of persons who are said to be fortunate or unfortunate? How comes it that this opinion should prevail amongst men, if it be not justified by experience?"

"It is not for me to dispute with your majesty," replied the prudent vizier.

"Speak your mind freely; I desire and command it," said the sultan.

"Then I am of opinion," answered the vizier, "that people are often led to believe others fortunate, or unfortunate, merely because they only know the general outline of their histories; and are ignorant of the incidents and events in which they have shown prudence or imprudence. I have heard, for instance, that there are at present, in this city, two men, who are remarkable for their good and bad fortune: one is called Murad the Unlucky, and the other Saladin the Lucky. Now, I am inclined to think, if we could hear their stories, we should find that one is a prudent and the other an imprudent character."

"Where do these men live?" interrupted the sultan. "I will hear their histories from their own lips before I sleep."

"Murad the Unlucky lives in the next square," said the vizier.

The sultan desired to go thither immediately. Scarcely had they entered the square, when they heard the cry of loud lamentations. They followed the sound till they came to a house of which the door was open, and where there was a man tearing his turban, and weeping bitterly. They asked the cause of his distress, and he pointed to the fragments of a china vase, which lay on the pavement at his door.

"This seems undoubtedly to be beautiful china," said the sultan, taking up one of the broken pieces; "but can the loss of a china vase be the cause of such violent grief and despair?"

"Ah, gentlemen," said the owner of the vase, suspending his lamentations, and looking at the dress of the pretended merchants, "I see that you are strangers: you do not know how much cause I have for grief and despair! You do not know that you are speaking to Murad the Unlucky! Were you to hear all the unfortunate accidents that have happened to me, from the time I was born till this instant, you would perhaps pity me, and acknowledge I have just cause for despair."

Curiosity was strongly expressed by the sultan; and the hope of obtaining sympathy inclined Murad to gratify it by the recital of his adventures. "Gentlemen," said he, "I scarcely dare invite you into the house of such an unlucky being as I am; but if you will venture to take a night's lodging under my roof, you shall hear at your leisure the story of my misfortunes."

The sultan and the vizier excused themselves from spending the night with Murad, saying that they were obliged to proceed to their khan, where they should be expected by their companions; but they begged permission to repose themselves for half an hour in his house, and besought him to relate the history of his life, if it would not renew his grief too much to recollect his misfortunes.

Few men are so miserable as not to like to talk of their misfortunes, where they have, or where they think they have, any chance of obtaining compassion. As soon as the pretended merchants were seated, Murad began his story in the following manner:—

"My father was a merchant of this city. The night before I was born he dreamed that I came into the world with the head of a dog and the tail of a dragon; and that, in haste to conceal my deformity, he rolled me up in a piece of linen, which unluckily proved to be the grind seignior's turban; who, enraged at his insolence in touching his turban, commanded that his head should be struck off.

"My father awaked before he lost his head, but not before he had lost half his wits from the terror of his dream. He considered it as a warning sent from above, and consequently determined to avoid the sight of me. He would not stay to see whether I should really be born with the head of a dog and the tail of a dragon; but he set out, the next morning, on a voyage to Aleppo.

"He was absent for upwards of seven years; and during that time my education was totally neglected. One day I inquired from my mother why I had been named Murad the Unlucky. She told me that this name was given to me in consequence of my father's dream; but she added that perhaps it might be forgotten, if I proved fortunate in my future life. My nurse, a very old woman, who was present, shook her head, with a look which I shall never forget, and whispered to my mother loud enough for me to hear, 'Unlucky he was, and is, and ever will be. Those that are born to ill luck cannot help themselves; nor can any, but the great prophet, Mahomet himself, do anything for them. It is a folly for an unlucky person to strive with their fate: it is better to yield to it at once.'

"This speech made a terrible impression upon me, young as I then was; and every accident that happened to me afterwards confirmed my belief in my nurse's prognostic. I was in my eighth year when my father returned from abroad. The year after he came home my brother Saladin was born, who was named Saladin the Lucky, because the day he was born a vessel freighted with rich merchandise for my father arrived safely in port.

"I will not weary you with a relation of all the little instances of good fortune by which my brother Saladin was distinguished, even during his childhood. As he grew up, his success in everything he undertook was as remarkable as my ill luck in all that I attempted. From the time the rich vessel arrived, we lived in splendour; and the supposed prosperous state of my father's affairs was of course attributed to the influence of my brother Saladin's happy destiny.

"When Saladin was about twenty, my father was taken dangerously ill; and as he felt that he should not recover, he sent for my brother to the side of his bed, and, to his great surprise, informed him that the magnificence in which we had lived had exhausted all his wealth; that his affairs were in the greatest disorder; for, having trusted to the hope of continual success, he had embarked in projects beyond his powers.

"The sequel was, he had nothing remaining to leave to his children but two large china vases, remarkable for their beauty, but still more valuable on account of certain verses inscribed upon them in an unknown character, which were supposed to operate as a talisman or charm in favour of their possessors.

"Both these vases my father bequeathed to my brother Saladin; declaring he could not venture to leave either of them to me, because I was so unlucky that I should inevitably break it. After his death, however, my brother Saladin, who was blessed with a generous temper, gave me my choice of the two vases; and endeavoured to raise my spirits by repeating frequently that he had no faith either in good fortune or ill fortune.

"I could not be of his opinion, though I felt and acknowledged his kindness in trying to persuade me out of my settled melancholy. I knew it was in vain for me to exert myself, because I was sure that, do what I would, I should still be Murad the Unlucky. My brother, on the contrary, was nowise cast down, even by the poverty in which my father left us: he said he was sure he should find some means of maintaining himself; and so he did.

"On examining our china vases, he found in them a powder of a bright scarlet colour; and it occurred to him that it would make a fine dye. He tried it, and after some trouble, it succeeded to admiration.

"During my father's lifetime, my mother had been supplied with rich dresses by one of the merchants who was employed by the ladies of the grand seignior's seraglio. My brother had done this merchant some trifling favours, and, upon application to him, he readily engaged to recommend the new scarlet dye. Indeed, it was so beautiful, that, the moment it was seen, it was preferred to every other colour. Saladin's shop was soon crowded with customers; and his winning manners and pleasant conversation were almost as advantageous to him as his scarlet dye. On the contrary, I observed that the first glance at my melancholy countenance was sufficient to disgust every one who saw me. I perceived this plainly; and it only confirmed me the more in my belief in my own evil destiny.

"It happened one day that a lady, richly apparelled and attended by two female slaves, came to my brother's house to make some purchases. He was out, and I alone was left to attend to the shop. After she had looked over some goods, she chanced to see my china vase, which was in the room. She took a prodigious fancy to it, and offered me any price if I would part with it; but this I declined doing, because I believed that I should draw down upon my head some dreadful calamity if I voluntarily relinquished the talisman. Irritated by my refusal, the lady, according to the custom of her sex, became more resolute in her purpose; but neither entreaties nor money could change my determination. Provoked beyond measure at my obstinacy, as she called it, she left the house.

"On my brother's return, I related to him what had happened, and expected that he would have praised me for my prudence; but, on the contrary, he blamed me for the superstitious value I set upon the verses on my vase; and observed that it would be the height of folly to lose a certain means of advancing my fortune for the uncertain hope of magical protection. I could not bring myself to be of his opinion; I had not the courage to follow the advice he gave. The next day the lady returned, and my brother sold his vase to her for ten thousand pieces of gold. This money he laid out in the most advantageous manner, by purchasing a new stock of merchandise. I repented when it was too late; but I believe it is part of the fatality attending certain persons, that they cannot decide rightly at the proper moment. When the opportunity has been lost, I have always regretted that I did not do exactly the contrary to what I had previously determined upon. Often, whilst I was hesitating, the favourable moment passed. {1} Now this is what I call being unlucky. But to proceed with my story.

"The lady who bought my brother Saladin's vase was the favourite of the Sultan, and all-powerful in the seraglio. Her dislike to me, in consequence of my opposition to her wishes, was so violent, that she refused to return to my brother's house while I remained there. He was unwilling to part with me; but I could not bear to be the ruin of so good a brother. Without telling him my design, I left his house careless of what should become of me. Hunger, however, soon compelled me to think of some immediate mode of obtaining relief. I sat down upon a stone, before the door of a baker's shop: the smell of hot bread tempted me in, and with a feeble voice I demanded charity.

"The master baker gave me as much bread as I could eat, upon condition that I should change dresses with him and carry the rolls for him through the city this day. To this I readily consented; but I had soon reason to repent of my compliance. Indeed, if my ill-luck had not, as usual, deprived me at this critical moment of memory and judgment, I should never have complied with the baker's treacherous proposal. For some time before, the people of Constantinople had been much dissatisfied with the weight and quality of the bread furnished by the bakers. This species of discontent has often been the sure forerunner of an insurrection; and, in these disturbances, the master bakers frequently lose their lives. All these circumstances I knew, but they did not occur to my memory when they might have been useful.

"I changed dresses with the baker; but scarcely had I proceeded through the adjoining streets with my rolls before the mob began to gather round me with reproaches and execrations. The crowd pursued me even to the gates of the grand seignior's palace, and the grand vizier, alarmed at their violence, sent out an order to have my head struck off; the usual remedy, in such cases, being to strike off the baker's head.

"I now fell upon my knees, and protested I was not the baker for whom they took me; that I had no connection with him; and that I had never furnished the people of Constantinople with bread that was not weight. I declared I had merely changed clothes with a master baker for this day, and that I should not have done so but for the evil destiny which governs all my actions. Some of the mob exclaimed that I deserved to lose my head for my folly; but others took pity on me, and whilst the officer, who was sent to execute the vizier's order, turned to speak to some of the noisy rioters, those who were touched by my misfortune opened a passage for me through the crowd, and thus favoured, I effected my escape.

"I quitted Constantinople; my vase I had left in the care of my brother. At some miles' distance from the city I overtook a party of soldiers. I joined them, and learning that they were going to embark with the rest of the grand seignior's army for Egypt, I resolved to accompany them. 'If it be,' thought I, 'the will of Mahomet that I should perish, the sooner I meet my fate the better.' The despondency into which I was sunk was attended by so great a degree of indolence, that I scarcely would take the necessary means to preserve my existence. During our passage to Egypt I sat all day long upon the deck of the vessel, smoking my pipe, and I am convinced that if a storm had risen, as I expected, I should not have taken my pipe from my mouth, nor should I have handled a rope to save myself from destruction. Such is the effect of that species of resignation, or torpor, whichever you please to call it, to which my strong belief in fatality had reduced my mind.

"We landed, however, safely, contrary to my melancholy forebodings. By a trifling accident, not worth relating, I was detained longer than any of my companions in the vessel when we disembarked, and I did not arrive at the camp till late at night. It was moonlight, and I could see the whole scene distinctly. There was a vast number of small tents scattered over a desert of white sand; a few date-trees were visible at a distance; all was gloomy, and all still; no sound was to be heard but that of the camels feeding near the tents, and, as I walked on, I met with no human creature.

"My pipe was now out, and I quickened my pace a little towards a fire which I saw near one of the tents. As I proceeded, my eye was caught by something sparkling in the sand: it was a ring. I picked it up and put it on my finger, resolving to give it to the public crier the next morning, who might find out its rightful owner; but, by ill-luck, I put it on my little finger, for which it was much too large, and as I hastened towards the fire to light my pipe, I dropped the ring. I stooped to search for it amongst the provender on which a mule was feeding, and the cursed animal gave me so violent a kick on the head that I could not help roaring aloud.

"My cries awakened those who slept in the tent near which the mule was feeding. Provoked at being disturbed, the soldiers were ready enough to think ill of me, and they took it for granted that I was a thief, who had stolen the ring I pretended to have just found. The ring was taken from me by force, and the next day I was bastinadoed for having found it; the officer persisting in the belief that stripes would make me confess where I had concealed certain other articles of value which had lately been missed in the camp. All this was the consequence of my being in a hurry to light my pipe and of my having put the ring on a finger that was too little for it, which no one but Murad the Unlucky would have done.

"When I was able to walk again, after my wounds were healed, I went into one of the tents distinguished by a red flag, having been told that these were coffee-houses. Whilst I was drinking coffee I heard a stranger near me complaining that he had not been able to recover a valuable ring he had lost, although he had caused his loss to be published for three days by the public crier, offering a reward of two hundred sequins to whoever should restore it. I guessed that this was the very ring which I had unfortunately found. I addressed myself to the stranger, and promised to point out to him the person who had forced it from me. The stranger recovered his ring, and, being convinced that I had acted honestly, he made me a present of two hundred sequins, as some amends for the punishment which I had unjustly suffered on his account.

"Now you would imagine that this purse of gold was advantageous to me. Far the contrary; it was the cause of new misfortunes.

"One night, when I thought that the soldiers who were in the same tent with me were all fast asleep, I indulged myself in the pleasure of counting my treasure. The next day I was invited by my companions to drink sherbet with them. What they mixed with the sherbet which I drank I know not, but I could not resist the drowsiness it brought on. I fell into a profound slumber, and when I awoke, I found myself lying under a date-tree, at some distance from the camp.

"The first thing I thought of when I came to my recollection was my purse of sequins. The purse I found still safe in my girdle; but on opening it, I perceived that it was filled with pebbles, and not a single sequin was left. I had no doubt that I had been robbed by the soldiers with whom I had drunk sherbet, and I am certain that some of them must have been awake the night I counted my money; otherwise, as I had never trusted the secret of my riches to any one, they could not have suspected me of possessing any property; for ever since I kept company with them I had appeared to be in great indigence.

"I applied in vain to the superior officers for redress: the soldiers protested they were innocent; no positive proof appeared against them, and I gained nothing by my complaint but ridicule and ill-will. I called myself, in the first transport of my grief, by that name which, since my arrival in Egypt, I had avoided to pronounce: I called myself Murad the Unlucky. The name and the story ran through the camp, and I was accosted, afterwards, very frequently, by this appellation. Some, indeed, varied their wit by calling me Murad with the purse of pebbles.

"All that I had yet suffered is nothing compared to my succeeding misfortunes.

"It was the custom at this time, in the Turkish camp, for the soldiers to amuse themselves with firing at a mark. The superior officers remonstrated against this dangerous practice, but ineffectually. Sometimes a party of soldiers would stop firing for a few minutes, after a message was brought them from their commanders, and then they would begin again, in defiance of all orders. Such was the want of discipline in our army, that this disobedience went unpunished. In the meantime, the frequency of the danger made most men totally regardless of it. I have seen tents pierced with bullets, in which parties were quietly seated smoking their pipes, whilst those without were preparing to take fresh aim at the red flag on the top.

"This apathy proceeded, in some, from unconquerable indolence of body; in others, from the intoxication produced by the fumes of tobacco and of opium; but in most of my brother Turks it arose from the confidence which the belief in predestination inspired. When a bullet killed one of their companions, they only observed, scarcely taking the pipes from their mouths, 'Our hour is not yet come: it is not the will of Mahomet that we should fall.'

"I own that this rash security appeared to me, at first, surprising, but it soon ceased to strike me with wonder, and it even tended to confirm my favourite opinion, that some were born to good and some to evil fortune. I became almost as careless as my companions, from following the same course of reasoning. 'It is not,' thought I, 'in the power of human prudence to avert the stroke of destiny. I shall perhaps die to-morrow; let me therefore enjoy to-day.'

"I now made it my study every day to procure as much amusement as possible. My poverty, as you will imagine, restricted me from indulgence and excess, but I soon found means to spend what did not actually belong to me. There were certain Jews who were followers of the camp, and who, calculating on the probability of victory for our troops, advanced money to the soldiers, for which they engaged to pay these usurers exorbitant interest. The Jew to whom I applied traded with me also, upon the belief that my brother Saladin, with whose character and circumstances he was acquainted, would pay my debts if I should fall. With the money I raised from the Jew I continually bought coffee and opium, of which I grew immoderately fond. In the delirium it created I forgot all my misfortunes, all fear of the future.

"One day, when I had raised my spirits by an unusual quantity of opium, I was strolling through the camp, sometimes singing, sometimes dancing, like a madman, and repeating that I was not now Murad the Unlucky. Whilst these words were on my lips, a friendly spectator, who was in possession of his sober senses, caught me by the arm, and attempted to drag me from the place where I was exposing myself. 'Do you not see,' said he, 'those soldiers, who are firing at a mark? I saw one of them, just now, deliberately taking aim at your turban; and observe, he is now reloading his piece.' My ill luck prevailed even at this instant—the only instant in my life when I defied its power. I struggled with my adviser, repeating, 'I am not the wretch you take me for; I am not Murad the Unlucky.' He fled from the danger himself; I remained, and in a few seconds afterwards a ball reached me, and I fell senseless on the sand.

"The ball was cut out of my body by an awkward surgeon, who gave me ten times more pain than was necessary. He was particularly hurried at this time, because the army had just received orders to march in a few hours, and all was confusion in the camp. My wound was excessively painful, and the fear of being left behind with those who were deemed incurable added to my torments. Perhaps, if I had kept myself quiet, I might have escaped some of the evils I afterwards endured; but, as I have repeatedly told you, gentlemen, it was my ill fortune never to be able to judge what was best to be done till the time for prudence was past.

"During the day, when my fever was at the height, and when my orders were to keep my bed, contrary to my natural habits of indolence, I rose a hundred times, and went out of my tent in the very heat of the day, to satisfy my curiosity as to the number of the tests which had not been struck, and of the soldiers who had not yet marched. The orders to march were tardily obeyed, and many hours elapsed before our encampment was raised. Had I submitted to my surgeon's orders, I might have been in a state to accompany the most dilatory of the stragglers; I could have borne, perhaps, the slow motion of a litter, on which some of the sick were transported; but in the evening, when the surgeon came to dress my wounds, he found me in such a situation that it was scarcely possible to remove me.

"He desired a party of soldiers, who were left to bring up the rear, to call for me the next morning. They did so; but they wanted to put me upon the mule which I recollected, by a white streak on its back, to be the cursed animal that had kicked me whilst I was looking for the ring. I could not be prevailed upon to go upon this unlucky animal. I tried to persuade the soldiers to carry me, and they took me a little way; but, soon growing weary of their burden, they laid me down on the sand, pretending that they were going to fill a skin with water at a spring they had discovered, and bade me lie still, and wait for their return.

"I waited and waited, longing for the water to moisten my parched lips; but no water came—no soldiers returned; and there I lay, for several hours, expecting every moment to breathe my last. I made no effort to move, for I was now convinced my hour was come, and that it was the will of Mahomet that I should perish in this miserable manner, and lie unburied like a dog: 'a death,' thought I, 'worthy of Murad the Unlucky.'

"My forebodings were not this time just; a detachment of English soldiers passed near the place where I lay: my groans were heard by them, and they humanely came to my assistance. They carried me with them, dressed my wound, and treated me with the utmost tenderness. Christians though they were, I must acknowledge that I had reason to love them better than any of the followers of Mahomet, my good brother only excepted.

"Under their care I recovered; but scarcely had I regained my strength before I fell into new disasters. It was hot weather, and my thirst was excessive. I went out with a party, in hopes of finding a spring of water. The English soldiers began to dig for a well, in a place pointed out to them by one of their men of science. I was not inclined to such hard labour, but preferred sauntering on in search of a spring. I saw at a distance something that looked like a pool of water; and I pointed it out to my companions. Their man of science warned me by his interpreter not to trust to this deceitful appearance; for that such were common in this country, and that, when I came close to the spot, I should find no water there. He added, that it was at a greater distance than I imagined; and that I should, in all probability, be lost in the desert if I attempted to follow this phantom.

"I was so unfortunate as not to attend to his advice: I set out in pursuit of this accursed delusion, which assuredly was the work of evil spirits, who clouded my reason, and allured me into their dominion. I went on, hour after hour, in expectation continually of reaching the object of my wishes; but it fled faster than I pursued, and I discovered at last that the Englishman, who had doubtless gained his information from the people of the country, was right; and that the shining appearance which I had taken for water was a mere deception.

"I was now exhausted with fatigue: I looked back in vain after the companions I had left; I could see neither men, animals, nor any trace of vegetation in the sandy desert. I had no resource but, weary as I was, to measure back my footsteps, which were imprinted in the sand.

"I slowly and sorrowfully traced them as my guides in this unknown land. Instead of yielding to my indolent inclinations, I ought, however, to have made the best of my way back, before the evening breeze sprang up. I felt the breeze rising, and, unconscious of my danger, I rejoiced, and opened my bosom to meet it; but what was my dismay when I saw that the wind swept before it all trace of my footsteps in the sand. I knew not which way to proceed; I was struck with despair, tore my garments, threw off my turban, and cried aloud; but neither human voice nor echo answered me. The silence was dreadful. I had tasted no food for many hours, and I now became sick and faint. I recollected that I had put a supply of opium into the folds of my turban; but, alas! when I took my turban up, I found that the opium had fallen out. I searched for it in vain on the sand, where I had thrown the turban.

"I stretched myself out upon the ground, and yielded without further struggle to my evil destiny. What I suffered from thirst, hunger, and heat cannot be described. At last I fell into a sort of trance, during which images of various kinds seemed to flit before my eyes. How long I remained in this state I know not: but I remember that I was brought to my senses by a loud shout, which came from persons belonging to a caravan returning from Mecca. This was a shout of joy for their safe arrival at a certain spring, well known to them in this part of the desert.

"The spring was not a hundred yards from the spot where I lay; yet, such had been the fate of Murad the Unlucky, that he missed the reality, whilst he had been hours in pursuit of the phantom. Feeble and spiritless as I was, I sent forth as loud a cry as I could, in hopes of obtaining assistance; and I endeavoured to crawl to the place from which the voices appeared to come. The caravan rested for a considerable time whilst the slaves filled the skins with water, and whilst the camels took in their supply. I worked myself on towards them; yet, notwithstanding my efforts, I was persuaded that, according to my usual ill-fortune, I should never be able to make them hear my voice. I saw them mount their camels! I took off my turban, unrolled it, and waved it in the air. My signal was seen! The caravan came towards me!

"I had scarcely strength to speak; a slave gave me some water, and, after I had drunk, I explained to them who I was, and how I came into this situation.

"Whilst I was speaking, one of the travellers observed the purse which hung to my girdle: it was the same the merchant for whom I recovered the ring had given to me; I had carefully preserved it, because the initials of my benefactor's name and a passage from the Koran were worked upon it. When he give it to me, he said that perhaps we should meet again in some other part of the world, and he should recognise me by this token. The person who now took notice of the purse was his brother; and when I related to him how I had obtained it, he had the goodness to take me under his protection. He was a merchant, who was now going with the caravan to Grand Cairo: he offered to take me with him, and I willingly accepted the proposal, promising to serve him as faithfully as any of his slaves. The caravan proceeded, and I was carried with it."

CHAPTER II

"The merchant, who was become my master, treated me with great kindness; but on hearing me relate the whole series of my unfortunate adventures, he exacted a promise from me that I would do nothing without first consulting him. 'Since you are so unlucky, Murad,' said he, 'that you always choose for the worst when you choose for yourself, you should trust entirely to the judgment of a wiser or a more fortunate friend.'

"I fared well in the service of this merchant, who was a man of a mild disposition, and who was so rich that he could afford to be generous to all his dependants. It was my business to see his camels loaded and unloaded at proper places, to count his bales of merchandise, and to take care that they were not mixed with those of his companions. This I carefully did till the day we arrived at Alexandria; when, unluckily, I neglected to count the bales, taking it for granted that they were all right, as I had found them so the preceding day. However, when we were to go on board the vessel that was to take us to Cairo, I perceived that three bales of cotton were missing.

"I ran to inform my master, who, though a good deal provoked at my negligence, did not reproach me as I deserved. The public crier was immediately sent round the city, to offer a reward for the recovery of the merchandise; and it was restored by one of the merchants' slaves with whom we had travelled. The vessel was now under sail; my master and I and the bales of cotton were obliged to follow in a boat; and when we were taken on board, the captain declared he was so loaded, that he could not tell where to stow the bales of cotton. After much difficulty, he consented to let them remain upon deck; and I promised my master to watch them night and day.

"We had a prosperous voyage, and were actually in sight of shore, which the captain said we could not fail to reach early the next morning. I stayed, as usual, this night upon deck, and solaced myself by smoking my pipe. Ever since I had indulged in this practice at the camp at El Arish, I could not exist without opium and tobacco. I suppose that my reason was this night a little clouded with the dose I took; but towards midnight I was sobered by terror. I started up from the deck on which I had stretched myself; my turban was in flames—the bale of cotton on which I had rested was all on fire. I awakened two sailors, who were fast asleep on deck. The consternation became general, and the confusion increased the danger. The captain and my master were the most active, and suffered the most, in extinguishing the flames—my master was terribly scorched.

"For my part, I was not suffered to do anything; the captain ordered that I should be bound to the mast; and when at last the flames were extinguished, the passengers, with one accord, besought him to keep me bound hand and foot, lest I should be the cause of some new disaster. All that had happened was, indeed, occasioned by my ill-luck. I had laid my pipe down, when I was falling asleep, upon the bale of cotton that was beside me. The fire from my pipe fell out and set the cotton in flames. Such was the mixture of rage and terror with which I had inspired the whole crew, that I am sure they would have set me ashore on a desert island rather than have had me on board for a week longer. Even my humane master, I could perceive, was secretly impatient to get rid of Murad the Unlucky and his evil fortune.

"You may believe that I was heartily glad when we landed, and when I was unbound. My master put a purse containing fifty sequins into my hand, and bade me farewell. 'Use this money prudently, Murad, if you can,' said he, 'and perhaps your fortune may change.' Of this I had little hopes, but determined to lay out my money as prudently as possible.

"As I was walking through the streets of Grand Cairo, considering how I should lay out my fifty sequins to the greatest advantage, I was stopped by one who called me by my name, and asked me if I could pretend to have forgotten his face. I looked steadily at him, and recollected to my sorrow that he was the Jew Rachub, from whom I had borrowed certain sums of money at the camp at El Arish. What brought him to Grand Cairo, except it was my evil destiny, I cannot tell. He would not quit me; he would take no excuses; he said he knew that I had deserted twice, once from the Turkish and once from the English army; that I was not entitled to any pay; and that he could not imagine it possible that my brother Saladin would own me or pay my debts.

"I replied, for I was vexed by the insolence of this Jewish dog, that I was not, as he imagined, a beggar: that I had the means of paying him my just debt, but that I hoped he would not extort from me all that exorbitant interest which none but a Jew could exact. He smiled, and answered that if a Turk loved opium better than money this was no fault of his; that he had supplied me with what I loved best in the world, and that I ought not to complain when he expected I should return the favour.

"I will not weary you, gentlemen, with all the arguments that passed between me and Rachub. At last we compromised matters; he would take nothing less than the whole debt: but he let me have at a very cheap rate a chest of second-hand clothes, by which he assured me I might make my fortune. He brought them to Grand Cairo, he said, for the purpose of selling them to slave merchants, who, at this time of the year, were in want of them to supply their slaves; but he was in haste to get home to his wife and family at Constantinople, and, therefore, he was willing to make over to a friend the profits of this speculation. I should have distrusted Rachub's professions of friendship, and especially of disinterestedness, but he took me with him to the khan where his goods were, and unlocked the chest of clothes to show them to me. They were of the richest and finest materials, and had been but little worn. I could not doubt the evidence of my senses; the bargain was concluded, and the Jew sent porters to my inn with the chest.

"The next day I repaired to the public market-place; and, when my business was known, I had choice of customers before night—my chest was empty, and my purse was full. The profit I made upon the sale of these clothes was so considerable, that I could not help feeling astonishment at Rachub's having brought himself so readily to relinquish them.

"A few days after I had disposed of the contents of my chest, a Damascene merchant, who had bought two suits of apparel from me, told me, with a very melancholy face, that both the female slaves who had put on these clothes were sick. I could not conceive that the clothes were the cause of their sickness; but soon afterwards, as I was crossing the market, I was attacked by at least a dozen merchants, who made similar complaints. They insisted upon knowing how I came by the garments, and demanded whether I had worn any of them myself. This day I had, for the first time, indulged myself with wearing a pair of yellow slippers, the only finery I had reserved for myself out of all the tempting goods. Convinced by my wearing these slippers that I could have had no insidious designs, since I shared the danger, whatever it might be, the merchants were a little pacified; but what was my terror and remorse the next day, when one of them came to inform me that plague-boils had broken out under the arms of all the slaves who had worn this pestilential apparel! On looking carefully into the chest, we found the word 'Smyrna' written, and half effaced, upon the lid. Now, the plague had for some time raged at Smyrna; and, as the merchants suspected, these clothes had certainly belonged to persons who had died of that distemper. This was the reason why the Jew was willing to sell them to me so cheap; and it was for this reason that he would not stay at Grand Cairo himself to reap the profits of his speculation. Indeed, if I had paid attention to it at the proper time, a slight circumstance might have revealed the truth to me. Whilst I was bargaining with the Jew, before he opened the chest, he swallowed a large dram of brandy, and stuffed his nostrils with sponge dipped in vinegar; he told me, he did to prevent his perceiving the smell of musk, which always threw him into convulsions.

"The horror I felt when I discovered that I had spread the infection of the plague, and that I had probably caught it myself, overpowered my senses—a cold dew spread over all my limbs, and I fell upon the lid of the fatal chest in a swoon. It is said that fear disposes people to take the infection; however this may be, I sickened that evening, and soon was in a raging fever. It was worse for me whenever the delirium left me, and I could reflect upon the miseries my ill-fortune had occasioned. In my first lucid interval I looked round, and saw that I had been removed from the khan to a wretched hut. An old woman, who was smoking her pipe in the farthest corner of my room, informed me that I had been sent out of the town of Grand Cairo by order of the cadi, to whom the merchants had made their complaint. The fatal chest was burnt, and the house in which I had lodged razed to the ground. 'And if it had not been for me,' continued the old woman, 'you would have been dead probably at this instant; but I have made a vow to our great Prophet that I would never neglect an opportunity of doing a good action; therefore, when you were deserted by all the world, I took care of you. Here, too, is your purse, which I saved from the rabble—and, what is more difficult, from the officers of justice. I will account to you for every part that I have expended; and will, moreover, tell you the reason of my making such an extraordinary vow.'

"As I believed that this benevolent old woman took great pleasure in talking, I made an inclination of my head to thank her for her promised history, and she proceeded; but I must confess I did not listen with all the attention her narrative doubtless deserved. Even curiosity, the strongest passion of us Turks, was dead within me. I have no recollection of the old woman's story. It is as much as I can do to finish my own.

"The weather became excessively hot; it was affirmed by some of the physicians that this heat would prove fatal to their patients; but, contrary to the prognostics of the physicians, it stopped the progress of the plague. I recovered, and found my purse much lightened by my illness. I divided the remainder of my money with my humane nurse, and sent her out into the city to inquire how matters were going on.

"She brought me word that the fury of the plague had much abated, but that she had met several funerals, and that she had heard many of the merchants cursing the folly of Murad the Unlucky, who, as they said, had brought all this calamity upon the inhabitants of Cairo. Even fools, they say, learn by experience. I took care to burn the bed on which I had lain and the clothes I had worn; I concealed my real name, which I knew would inspire detestation, and gained admittance, with a crowd of other poor wretches, into a lazaretto, where I performed quarantine and offered up prayers daily for the sick.

"When I thought it was impossible I could spread the infection, I took my passage home. I was eager to get away from Grand Cairo, where I knew I was an object of execration. I had a strange fancy haunting my mind; I imagined that all my misfortunes, since I left Constantinople, had arisen from my neglect of the talisman upon the beautiful china vase. I dreamed three times, when I was recovering from the plague, that a genius appeared to me, and said, in a reproachful tone, 'Murad, where is the vase that was entrusted to thy care?'

"This dream operated strongly upon my imagination. As soon as we arrived at Constantinople, which we did, to my great surprise, without meeting with any untoward accidents, I went in search of my brother Saladin to inquire for my vase. He no longer lived in the house in which I left him, and I began to be apprehensive that he was dead, but a porter, hearing my inquiries, exclaimed, 'Who is there in Constantinople that is ignorant of the dwelling of Saladin the Lucky? Come with me, and I will show it to you.'

"The mansion to which he conducted me looked so magnificent that I was almost afraid to enter lest there should be some mistake. But whilst I was hesitating the doors opened, and I heard my brother Saladin's voice. He saw me almost at the same instant that I fixed my eyes upon him, and immediately sprang forward to embrace me. He was the same good brother as ever, and I rejoiced in his prosperity with all my heart. 'Brother Saladin,' said I, 'can you now doubt that some men are born to be fortunate and others to be unfortunate? How often you used to dispute this point with me!'

"'Let us not dispute it now in the public street,' said he, smiling; 'but come in and refresh yourself, and we will consider the question afterwards at leisure.'

"'No, my dear brother,' said I, drawing back, 'you are too good: Murad the Unlucky shall not enter your house, lest he should draw down misfortunes upon you and yours. I come only to ask for my vase.'

"'It is safe,' cried he; 'come in, and you shall see it: but I will not give it up till I have you in my house. I have none of these superstitious fears: pardon me the expression, but I have none of these superstitious fears.'

"I yielded, entered his house, and was astonished at all I saw. My brother did not triumph in his prosperity; but, on the contrary, seemed intent only upon making me forget my misfortunes: he listened to the account of them with kindness, and obliged me by the recital of his history: which was, I must acknowledge, far less wonderful than my own. He seemed, by his own account, to have grown rich in the common course of things; or rather, by his own prudence. I allowed for his prejudices, and, unwilling to dispute farther with him, said, 'You must remain of your opinion, brother, and I of mine; you are Saladin the Lucky, and I Murad the Unlucky; and so we shall remain to the end of our lives.'

"I had not been in his house four days when an accident happened, which showed how much I was in the right. The favourite of the sultan, to whom he had formerly sold his china vase, though her charms were now somewhat faded by time, still retained her power and her taste for magnificence. She commissioned my brother to bespeak for her, at Venice, the most splendid looking-glass that money could purchase. The mirror, after many delays and disappointments, at length arrived at my brother's house. He unpacked it, and sent to let the lady know it was in perfect safety. It was late in the evening, and she ordered it should remain where it was that night, and that it should be brought to the seraglio the next morning. It stood in a sort of ante-chamber to the room in which I slept; and with it were left some packages, containing glass chandeliers for an unfinished saloon in my brother's house. Saladin charged all his domestics to be vigilant this night, because he had money to a great amount by him, and there had been frequent robberies in our neighbourhood. Hearing these orders, I resolved to be in readiness at a moment's warning. I laid my scimitar beside me upon a cushion, and left my door half open, that I might hear the slightest noise in the ante-chamber or the great staircase. About midnight I was suddenly awakened by a noise in the ante-chamber. I started up, seized my scimitar, and the instant I got to the door, saw, by the light of the lamp which was burning in the room, a man standing opposite to me, with a drawn sword in his hand. I rushed forward, demanding what he wanted, and received no answer; but seeing him aim at me with his scimitar, I gave him, as I thought, a deadly blow. At this instant I heard a great crash; and the fragments of the looking-glass, which I had shivered, fell at my feet. At the same moment something black brushed by my shoulder: I pursued it, stumbled over the packages of glass, and rolled over them down the stairs.

"My brother came out of his room to inquire the cause of all this disturbance; and when he saw the fine mirror broken, and me lying amongst the glass chandeliers at the bottom of the stairs, he could not forbear exclaiming, 'Well, brother! you are indeed Murad the Unlucky.'

"When the first emotion was over, he could not, however, forbear laughing at my situation. With a degree of goodness, which made me a thousand times more sorry for the accident, he came downstairs to help me up, gave me his hand, and said, 'Forgive me if I was angry with you at first. I am sure you did not mean to do me any injury; but tell me how all this has happened?'

"Whilst Saladin was speaking, I heard the same kind of noise which had alarmed me in the ante-chamber; but, on looking back, I saw only a black pigeon, which flew swiftly by me, unconscious of the mischief he had occasioned. This pigeon I had unluckily brought into the house the preceding day; and had been feeding and trying to tame it for my young nephews. I little thought it would be the cause of such disasters. My brother, though he endeavoured to conceal his anxiety from me, was much disturbed at the idea of meeting the favourite's displeasure, who would certainly be grievously disappointed by the loss of her splendid looking-glass. I saw that I should inevitably be his ruin if I continued in his house; and no persuasions could prevail upon me to prolong my stay. My generous brother, seeing me determined to go, said to me, 'A factor, whom I have employed for some years to sell merchandise for me, died a few days ago. Will you take his place? I am rich enough to bear any little mistakes you may fall into from ignorance of business; and you will have a partner who is able and willing to assist you.'

"I was touched to the heart by this kindness, especially at such a time as this. He sent one of his slaves with me to the shop in which you now see me, gentlemen. The slave, by my brother's directions, brought with us my china vase, and delivered it safely to me, with this message: 'The scarlet dye that was found in this vase, and in its fellow, was the first cause of Saladin's making the fortune he now enjoys: he therefore does no more than justice in sharing that fortune with his brother Murad.'

"I was now placed in as advantageous a situation as possible; but my mind was ill at ease when I reflected that the broken mirror might be my brother's ruin. The lady by whom it had been bespoken was, I well knew, of a violent temper; and this disappointment was sufficient to provoke her to vengeance. My brother sent me word this morning, however, that though her displeasure was excessive, it was in my power to prevent any ill consequences that might ensue. 'In my power!' I exclaimed; 'then, indeed, I am happy! Tell my brother there is nothing I will not do to show him my gratitude and to save him from the consequences of my folly.'

"The slave who was sent by my brother seemed unwilling to name what was required of me, saying that his master was afraid I should not like to grant the request. I urged him to speak freely, and he then told me the favourite declared nothing would make her amends for the loss of the mirror but the fellow-vase to that which she had bought from Saladin. It was impossible for me to hesitate; gratitude for my brother's generous kindness overcame my superstitious obstinacy, and I sent him word I would carry the vase to him myself.

"I took it down this evening from the shelf on which it stood; it was covered with dust, and I washed it, but, unluckily, in endeavouring to clean the inside from the remains of the scarlet powder, I poured hot water into it, and immediately I heard a simmering noise, and my vase, in a few instants, burst asunder with a loud explosion. These fragments, alas! are all that remain. The measure of my misfortunes is now completed! Can you wonder, gentlemen, that I bewail my evil destiny? Am I not justly called Murad the Unlucky? Here end all my hopes in this world! Better would it have been if I had died long ago! Better that I had never been born! Nothing I ever have done or attempted has prospered. Murad the Unlucky is my name, and ill-fate has marked me for her own."

CHAPTER III

The lamentations of Murad were interrupted by the entrance of Saladin. Having waited in vain for some hours, he now came to see if any disaster had happened to his brother Murad. He was surprised at the sight of the two pretended merchants, and could not refrain from exclamations on beholding the broken vase. However, with his usual equanimity and good- nature, he began to console Murad; and, taking up the fragments, examined them carefully, one by one joined them together again, found that none of the edges of the china were damaged, and declared he could have it mended so as to look as well as ever.

Murad recovered his spirits upon this. "Brother," said he, "I comfort myself for being Murad the Unlucky when I reflect that you are Saladin the Lucky. See, gentlemen," continued he, turning to the pretended merchants, "scarcely has this most fortunate of men been five minutes in company before he gives a happy turn to affairs. His presence inspires joy: I observe your countenances, which had been saddened by my dismal history, have brightened up since he has made his appearance. Brother, I wish you would make these gentlemen some amends for the time they have wasted in listening to my catalogue of misfortunes by relating your history, which, I am sure, they will find rather more exhilarating."

Saladin consented, on condition that the strangers would accompany him home and partake of a social banquet. They at first repeated the former excuse of their being obliged to return to their inn; but at length the sultan's curiosity prevailed, and he and his vizier went home with Saladin the Lucky, who, after supper, related his history in the following manner:—

"My being called Saladin the Lucky first inspired me with confidence in myself; though I own that I cannot remember any extraordinary instances of good luck in my childhood. An old nurse of my mother's, indeed, repeated to me twenty times a day that nothing I undertook could fail to succeed, because I was Saladin the Lucky. I became presumptuous and rash; and my nurse's prognostics might have effectually prevented their accomplishment had I not, when I was about fifteen, been roused to reflection during a long confinement, which was the consequence of my youthful conceit and imprudence.

"At this time there was at the Porte a Frenchman, an ingenious engineer, who was employed and favoured by the sultan, to the great astonishment of many of my prejudiced countrymen. On the grand seignior's birthday he exhibited some extraordinarily fine fireworks; and I, with numbers of the inhabitants of Constantinople, crowded to see them. I happened to stand near the place where the Frenchman was stationed; the crowd pressed upon him, and I amongst the rest; he begged we would, for our own sakes, keep at a greater distance, and warned us that we might be much hurt by the combustibles which he was using. I, relying upon my mood fortune, disregarded all these cautions; and the consequence was that, as I touched some of the materials prepared for the fireworks, they exploded, dashed me upon the ground with great violence, and I was terribly burnt.

"This accident, gentlemen, I consider as one of the most fortunate circumstances of my life; for it checked and corrected the presumption of my temper. During the time I was confined to my bed the French gentleman came frequently to see me. He was a very sensible man; and the conversations he had with me enlarged my mind and cured me of many foolish prejudices, especially of that which I had been taught to entertain concerning the predominance of what is called luck or fortune in human affairs. 'Though you are called Saladin the Lucky,' said he, 'you find that your neglect of prudence has nearly brought you to the grave even in the bloom of youth. Take my advice, and henceforward trust more to prudence than to fortune. Let the multitude, if they will, call you Saladin the Lucky; but call yourself, and make yourself, Saladin the Prudent.'

"These words left an indelible impression on my mind, and gave a new turn to my thoughts and character. My brother, Murad, his doubtless told you our difference of opinion on the subject of predestination produced between us frequent arguments; but we could never convince one another, and we each have acted, through life, in consequence of our different beliefs. To this I attribute my success and his misfortunes.

"The first rise of my fortune, as you have probably heard from Murad, was owing to the scarlet dye, which I brought to perfection with infinite difficulty. The powder, it is true, was accidentally found by me in our china vases; but there it might have remained to this instant, useless, if I had not taken the pains to make it useful. I grant that we can only partially foresee and command events; yet on the use we make of our own powers, I think, depends our destiny. But, gentlemen, you would rather hear my adventures, perhaps, than my reflections; and I am truly concerned, for your sakes, that I have no wonderful events to relate. I am sorry I cannot tell you of my having been lost in a sandy desert. I have never had the plague, nor even been shipwrecked: I have been all my life an inhabitant of Constantinople, and have passed my time in a very quiet and uniform manner.

"The money I received from the sultan's favourite for my china vase, as my brother may have told you, enabled me to trade on a more extensive scale. I went on steadily with my business, and made it my whole study to please my employers by all fair and honourable means. This industry and civility succeeded beyond my expectations: in a few years I was rich for a man in my way of business.

"I will not proceed to trouble you with the journal of a petty merchant's life; I pass on to the incident which made a considerable change in my affairs.

"A terrible fire broke out near the walls of the grand seignior's seraglio. As you are strangers, gentlemen, you may not have heard of this event, though it produced so great a sensation in Constantinople. The vizier's superb palace was utterly consumed, and the melted lead poured down from the roof of the mosque of St. Sophia. Various were the opinions formed by my neighbours respecting the cause of the conflagration. Some supposed it to be a punishment for the sultan's having neglected one Friday to appear it the mosque of St. Sophia; others considered it as a warning sent by Mahomet to dissuade the Porte from persisting in a war in which we were just engaged. The generality, however, of the coffee-house politicians contented themselves with observing that it was the will of Mahomet that the palace should be consumed. Satisfied by this supposition, they took no precaution to prevent similar accidents in their own houses. Never were fires so common in the city as at this period; scarcely a night passed without our being wakened by the cry of fire.

"These frequent fires were rendered still more dreadful by villains, who were continually on the watch to increase the confusion by which they profited, and to pillage the houses of the sufferers. It was discovered that these incendiaries frequently skulked, towards evening, in the neighbourhood of the bezestein, where the richest merchants store their goods. Some of these wretches were detected in throwing coundaks, or matches, into the windows; and if these combustibles remained a sufficient time, they could not fail to set the house on fire.

"Notwithstanding all these circumstances, many even of those who had property to preserve continued to repeat, 'It is the will of Mahomet,' and consequently to neglect all means of preservation. I, on the contrary, recollecting the lesson I had learned from the sensible foreigner, neither suffered my spirits to sink with superstitious fears of ill-luck, nor did I trust presumptuously to my good fortune. I took every possible means to secure myself. I never went to bed without having seen that all the lights and fires in the house were extinguished, and that I had a supply of water in the cistern. I had likewise learned from my Frenchman that wet mortar was the most effectual thing for stopping the progress of flames. I, therefore, had a quantity of mortar made up in one of my outhouses, which I could use at a moment's warning. These precautions were all useful to me. My own house, indeed, was never actually on fire; but the houses of my next-door neighbours were no less than five times in flames in the course of one winter. By my exertions, or rather by my precautions, they suffered but little damage, and all my neighbours looked upon me as their deliverer and friend; they loaded me with presents, and offered more, indeed, than I would accept. All repeated that I was Saladin the Lucky. This compliment I disclaimed, feeling more ambitious of being called Saladin the Prudent. It is thus that what we call modesty is often only a more refined species of pride. But to proceed with my story.

"One night I had been later than usual at supper at a friend's house; none but the watch were in the streets, and even they, I believe, were asleep.

"As I passed one of the conduits which convey water to the city, I heard a trickling noise; and, upon examination, I found that the cook of the water-spout was half turned, so that the water was running out. I turned it back to its proper place, thought it had been left unturned by accident, and walked on; but I had not proceeded far before I came to another spout, and another, which were in the same condition. I was convinced that this could not be the effect merely of accident, and suspected that some ill-intentioned persons designed to let out and waste the water of the city, that there might be none to extinguish any fire that should break out in the course of the night.

"I stood still for a few moments, to consider how it would be most prudent to act. It would be impossible for me to run to all parts of the city, that I might stop the pipes that were running to waste. I first thought of wakening the watch and the firemen, who were most of them slumbering at their stations; but I reflected that they were perhaps not to be trusted, and that they were in a confederacy with the incendiaries, otherwise they would certainly before this hour have observed and stopped the running of the sewers in their neighbourhood. I determined to waken a rich merchant, called Damat Zade, who lived near me, and who had a number of slaves whom he could send to different parts of the city, to prevent mischief and give notice to the inhabitants of their danger.

"He was a very sensible, active man, and one that could easily be wakened; he was not like some Turks, an hour in recovering their lethargic senses. He was quick in decision and action; and his slaves resembled their master. He despatched a messenger immediately to the grand vizier, that the sultan's safety might be secured, and sent others to the magistrates in each quarter of Constantinople. The large drums in the janissary aga's tower beat to rouse the inhabitants; and scarcely had they been heard to beat half an hour before the fire broke out in the lower apartments of Damat Zade's house, owing to a coundak which had been left behind one of the doors.

"The wretches who had prepared the mischief came to enjoy it, and to pillage; but they were disappointed. Astonished to find themselves taken into custody, they could not comprehend how their designs had been frustrated. By timely exertions, the fire in my friend's house was extinguished; and though fires broke out during the night in many parts of the city, but little damage was sustained, because there was time for precautions, and, by the stopping of the spouts, sufficient water was preserved. People were awakened and warned of the danger, and they consequently escaped unhurt.

"The next day, as soon as I made my appearance at the bezestein, the merchants crowded round, called me their benefactor, and the preserver of their lives and fortunes. Damat Zade, the merchant whom I had awakened the preceding night, presented to me a heavy purse of gold, and put upon my finger a diamond ring of considerable value; each of the merchants followed his example in making me rich presents; the magistrates also sent me tokens of their approbation; and the grand vizier sent me a diamond of the first water, with a line written by his own hand, 'To the man who has saved Constantinople.' Excuse me, gentlemen, for the vanity I seem to show in mentioning these circumstances. You desired to hear my history, and I cannot, therefore, omit the principal circumstance of my life. In the course of four-and-twenty hours I found myself raised, by the munificent gratitude of the inhabitants of this city, to a state of affluence far beyond what I had ever dreamed of attaining.

"I now took a house suited to my circumstances, and bought a few slaves. As I was carrying my slaves home, I was met by a Jew, who stopped me, saying, in his language, 'My lord, I see, has been purchasing slaves; I could clothe them cheaply.' There was something mysterious in the manner of this Jew, and I did not like his countenance; but I considered that I ought not to be governed by caprice in my dealings, and that, if this man could really clothe my slaves more cheaply than another, I ought not to neglect his offer merely because I took a dislike to the cut of his beard, the turn of his eye, or the tone of his voice. I, therefore, bade the Jew follow me home, saying that I would consider of his proposal.

"When we came to talk over the matter, I was surprised to find him so reasonable in his demands. On one point, indeed, he appeared unwilling to comply. I required not only to see the clothes I was offered, but also to know how they came into his possession. On this subject he equivocated; I, therefore, suspected there must be something wrong. I reflected what it could be, and judged that the goods had been stolen, or that they had been the apparel of persons who had died of some contagious distemper. The Jew showed me a chest, from which he said I might choose whatever suited me best. I observed that, as he was going to unlock the chest, he stuffed his nose with some aromatic herbs. He told me that he did so to prevent his smelling the musk with which the chest was perfumed; musk, he said, had an extraordinary effect upon his nerves. I begged to have some of the herbs which he used himself, declaring that musk was likewise offensive to me.

"The Jew, either struck by his own conscience or observing my suspicions, turned as pale as death. He pretended he had not the right key, and could not unlock the chest; said he must go in search of it, and that he would call on me again.

"After he had left me, I examined some writing upon the lid of the chest that had been nearly effaced. I made out the word 'Smyrna,' and this was sufficient to confirm all my suspicions. The Jew returned no more; he sent some porters to carry away the chest, and I heard nothing of him for some time, till one day, when I was at the house of Damat Zade, I saw a glimpse of the Jew passing hastily through one of the courts, as if he wished to avoid me. 'My friend,' said I to Damat Zade, 'do not attribute my question to impertinent curiosity, or to a desire to intermeddle with your affairs, if I venture to ask the nature of your business with the Jew who has just now crossed your court?'

"'He has engaged to supply me with clothing for my slaves,' replied my friend, 'cheaper than I can purchase it elsewhere. I have a design to surprise my daughter Fatima, on her birthday, with an entertainment in the pavilion in the garden, and all her female slaves shall appear in new dresses on the occasion.'

"I interrupted my friend, to tell him what I suspected relative to this Jew and his chest of clothes. It is certain that the infection of the plague can be communicated by clothes, not only after months, but after years have elapsed. The merchant resolved to have nothing more to do with this wretch, who could thus hazard the lives of thousands of his follow-creatures for a few pieces of gold. We sent notice of the circumstance to the cadi, but the cadi was slow in his operations; and before he could take the Jew into custody the cunning fellow had effected his escape. When his house was searched, he and his chest had disappeared. We discovered that he sailed for Egypt, and rejoiced that we had driven him from Constantinople.

"My friend, Damat Zade, expressed the warmest gratitude to me. 'You formerly saved my fortune; you have now saved my life, and a life yet dearer than my own: that of my daughter Fatima.'

"At the sound of that name I could not, I believe, avoid showing some emotion. I had accidentally seen this lady, and I had been captivated by her beauty and by the sweetness of her countenance; but as I knew she was destined to be the wife of another, I suppressed my feeling, and determined to banish the recollection of the fair Fatima for ever from my imagination. Her father, however, at this instant threw into my way a temptation which it required all my fortitude to resist. 'Saladin,' continued he, 'it is but just that you, who have saved our lives, should share our festivlty. Come here on the birthday of my Fatima; I will place you in a balcony which overlooks the garden, and you shall see the whole spectacle. We shall have a feast of tulips, in imitation of that which, as you know, is held in the grand seignior's gardens. I assure you the sight will be worth seeing; and besides, you will have a chance of beholding my Fatima, for a moment, without her veil.'

"'That,' interrupted I, 'is the thing I most wish to avoid. I dare not indulge myself in a pleasure which might cost me the happiness of my life. I will conceal nothing from you, who treat me with so much confidence. I have already beheld the charming countenance of your Fatima, but I know that she is destined to be the wife of a happier man.'

"Damat Zade seemed much pleased by the frankness with which I explained myself; but he would not give up the idea of my sitting with him in the balcony on the day of the feast of tulips; and I, on my part, could not consent to expose myself to another view of the charming Fatima. My friend used every argument, or rather every sort of persuasion, he could imagine to prevail upon me; he then tried to laugh me out of my resolution; and, when all failed, he said, in a voice of anger, 'Go, then, Saladin: I am sure you are deceiving me; you have a passion for some other woman, and you would conceal it from me, and persuade me you refuse the favour I offer you from prudence, when, in fact, it is from indifference and contempt. Why could you not speak the truth of your heart to me with that frankness with which one friend should treat another?'

"Astonished at this unexpected charge, and at the anger which flashed from the eyes of Damat Zade, who till this moment had always appeared to me a man of a mild and reasonable temper, I was for an instant tempted to fly into a passion and leave him; but friends, once lost, are not easily regained. This consideration had power sufficient to make me command my temper. 'My friend,' replied I, 'we will talk over this affair to-morrow. You are now angry, and cannot do me justice, but to-morrow you will be cool; you will then be convinced that I have not deceived you, and that I have no design but to secure my own happiness, by the most prudent means in my power, by avoiding the sight of the dangerous Fatima. I have no passion for any other woman.'

"'Then,' said my friend, embracing me, and quitting the tone of anger which he had assumed only to try my resolution to the utmost, 'Then, Saladin, Fatima is yours.'

"I scarcely dared to believe my senses; I could not express my joy! 'Yes, my friend,' continued the merchant, 'I have tried your prudence to the utmost, it has been victorious, and I resign my Fatima to you, certain that you will make her happy. It is true I had a greater alliance in view for her—the Pacha of Maksoud has demanded her from me; but I have found, upon private inquiry, he is addicted to the intemperate use of opium, and my daughter shall never be the wife of one who is a violent madman one-half the day and a melancholy idiot during the remainder. I have nothing to apprehend from the pacha's resentment, because I have powerful friends with the grand vizier, who will oblige him to listen to reason, and to submit quietly to a disappointment he so justly merits. And now, Saladin, have you any objection to seeing the feast of tulips?'

"I replied only by falling at the merchant's feet, and embracing his knees. The feast of tulips came and on that day I was married to the charming Fatima! The charming Fatima I continue still to think her, though she has now been my wife some years. She is the joy and pride of my heart; and, from our mutual affection, I have experienced more felicity than from all the other circumstances of my life, which are called so fortunate. Her father gave me the house in which I now live, and joined his possessions to ours; so that I have more wealth even than I desire. My riches, however, give me continually the means of relieving the wants of others; and therefore I cannot affect to despise them. I must persuade my brother Murad to share them with me, and to forget his misfortunes: I shall then think myself completely happy. As to the sultana's looking-glass and your broken vase, my dear brother," continued Saladin, "we must think of some means—"

"Think no more of the sultana's looking-glass or of the broken vase," exclaimed the sultan, throwing aside his merchant's habit, and showing beneath it his own imperial vest. "Saladin, I rejoice to have heard, from your own lips, the history of your life. I acknowledge, vizier, I have been in the wrong in our argument," continued the sultan, turning to his vizier. "I acknowledge that the histories of Saladin the Lucky and Murad the Unlucky favour your opinion, that prudence has more influence than chance in human affairs. The success and happiness of Saladin seem to me to have arisen from his prudence: by that prudence Constantinople has been saved from flames and from the plague. Had Murad possessed his brother's discretion, he would not have been on the point of losing his head, for selling rolls which he did not bake: he would not have been kicked by a mule or bastinadoed for finding a ring: he would not have been robbed by one party of soldiers, or shot by another: he would not have been lost in a desert, or cheated by a Jew: he would not have set a ship on fire; nor would he have caught the plague, and spread it through Grand Cairo: he would not have run my sultana's looking-glass through the body, instead of a robber: he would not have believed that the fate of his life depended on certain verses on a china vase: nor would he, at last, have broken this precious talisman, by washing it with hot water.

Henceforward, let Murad the Unlucky be named Murad the Imprudent: let Saladin preserve the surname he merits, and be henceforth called Saladin the Prudent."

So spake the sultan, who, unlike the generality of monarchs, could bear to find himself in the wrong, and could discover his vizier to be in the right without cutting off his head. History farther informs us that the sultan offered to make Saladin a pacha, and to commit to him the government of a province; but, Saladin the Prudent declined this honour, saying he had no ambition, was perfectly happy in his present situation, and that, when this was the case, it would be folly to change, because no one can be more than happy. What farther adventures befell Murad the Imprudent are not recorded; it is known only that he became a daily visitor to the Teriaky, and that he died a martyr to the immoderate use of opium.

THE LIMERICK GLOVES

CHAPTER I

It was Sunday morning, and a fine day in autumn; the bells of Hereford Cathedral rang, and all the world, smartly dressed, were flocking to church.

"Mrs. Hill! Mrs. Hill!—Phoebe! Phoebe! There's the cathedral bell, I say, and neither of you ready for church, and I a verger," cried Mr. Hill, the tanner, as he stood at the bottom of his own staircase. "I'm ready, papa," replied Phoebe; and down she came, looking so clean, so fresh, and so gay, that her stern father's brows unbent, and he could only say to her, as she was drawing on a new pair of gloves, "Child, you ought to have had those gloves on before this time of day."

"Before this time of day!" cried Mrs. Hill, who was now coming downstairs completely equipped— "before this time of day! She should know better, I say, than to put on those gloves at all: more especially when going to the cathedral."

"The gloves are very good gloves, as far as I see," replied Mr. Hill. "But no matter now. It is more fitting that we should be in proper time in our pew, to set an example, as becomes us, than to stand here talking of gloves and nonsense."

He offered his wife and daughter each an arm, and set out for the cathedral; but Phoebe was too busy in drawing on her new gloves, and her mother was too angry at the sight of them, to accept of Mr. Hill's courtesy. "What I say is always nonsense, I know, Mr. Hill," resumed the matron: "but I can see as far into a millstone as other folks. Was it not I that first gave you a hint of what became of the great dog that we lost out of our tan-yard last winter? And was it not I who first took notice to you, Mr. Hill, verger as you are, of the hole under the foundation of the cathedral? Was it not, I ask you, Mr. Hill?"

"But, my dear Mrs. Hill, what has all this to do with Phoebe's gloves?"

"Are you blind, Mr. Hill? Don't you see that they are Limerick gloves?"

"What of that?" said Mr. Hill, still preserving his composure, as it was his custom to do as long as he could, when he saw his wife was ruffled.

"What of that, Mr. Hill! why, don't you know that Limerick is in Ireland, Mr. Hill?"

"With all my heart, my dear."

"Yes, and with all your heart, I suppose, Mr. Hill, you would see our cathedral blown up, some fair day or other, and your own daughter married to the person that did it; and you a verger, Mr. Hill."

"God forbid!" cried Mr, Hill; and he stopped short and settled his wig. Presently recovering himself, he added, "But, Mrs. Hill, the cathedral is not yet blown up; and our Phoebe is not yet married."

"No; but what of that, Mr. Hill? Forewarned is forearmed, as I told you before your dog was gone; but you would not believe me, and you see how it turned out in that case; and so it will in this case, you'll see, Mr. Hill."

"But you puzzle and frighten me out of my wits, Mrs. Hill," said the verger, again settling his wig. "In that case and in this case! I can't understand a syllable of what you've been saying to me this half- hour. In plain English, what is there the matter about Phoebe's gloves?"

"In plain English, then, Mr. Hill, since you can understand nothing else, please to ask your daughter Phoebe who gave her those gloves. Phoebe, who gave you those gloves?"

"I wish they were burnt," said the husband, whose patience could endure no longer. "Who gave you those cursed gloves, Phoebe?"

"Papa," answered Phoebe, in a low voice, "they were a present from Mr. Brian O'Neill."

"The Irish glover!" cried Mr. Hill, with a look of terror.

"Yes," resumed the mother; "very true, Mr. Hill, I assure you. Now, you see, I had my reasons."

"Take off the gloves directly: I order you, Phoebe," said her father, in his most peremptory tone. "I took a mortal dislike to that Mr. Brian O'Neill the first time I ever saw him. He's an Irishman, and that's enough, and too much for me. Off with the gloves, Phoebe! When I order a thing, it must be done."

Phoebe seemed to find some difficulty in getting off the gloves, and gently urged that she could not well go into the cathedral without them. This objection was immediately removed by her mother's pulling from her pocket a pair of mittens, which had once been brown, and once been whole, but which were now rent in sundry places; and which, having been long stretched by one who was twice the size of Phoebe, now hung in huge wrinkles upon her well-turned arms.

"But, papa," said Phoebe, "why should we take a dislike to him because he is an Irishman? Cannot an Irishman be a good man?"

The verger made no answer to this question, but a few seconds after it was put to him observed that the cathedral bell had just done ringing; and, as they were now got to the church door, Mrs. Hill, with a significant look at Phoebe, remarked that it was no proper time to talk or think of good men, or bad men, or Irishmen, or any men, especially for a verger's daughter.

We pass over in silence the many conjectures that were made by several of the congregation concerning the reason why Miss Phoebe Hill should appear in such a shameful shabby pair of gloves on a Sunday. After service was ended, the verger went, with great mystery, to examine the hole under the foundation of the cathedral; and Mrs. Hill repaired, with the grocer's and the stationer's ladies, to take a walk in the Close, where she boasted to all her female acquaintance, whom she called her friends, of her maternal discretion in prevailing upon Mr. Hill to forbid her daughter Phoebe to wear the Limerick gloves.

In the meantime, Phoebe walked pensively homewards, endeavouring to discover why her father should take a mortal dislike to a man at first sight, merely because he was an Irishman: and why her mother had talked so much of the great dog which had been lost last year out of the tan-yard; and of the hole under the foundation of the cathedral! "What has all this to do with my Limerick gloves?" thought she. The more she thought, the less connection she could perceive between these things: for as she had not taken a dislike to Mr. Brian O'Neill at first sight, because he was an Irishman, she could not think it quite reasonable to suspect him of making away with her father's dog, nor yet of a design to blow up Hereford Cathedral. As she was pondering upon these matters, she came within sight of the ruins of a poor woman's house, which a few months before this time had been burnt down. She recollected that her first acquaintance with her lover began at the time of this fire; and she thought that the courage and humanity he showed, in exerting himself to save this unfortunate woman and her children, justified her notion of the possibility that an Irishman might be a good man.

The name of the poor woman whose house had been burnt down was Smith: she was a widow, and she now lived at the extremity of a narrow lane in a wretched habitation. Why Phoebe thought of her with more concern than usual at this instant we need not examine, but she did; and, reproaching herself for having neglected it for some weeks past, she resolved to go directly to see the widow Smith, and to give her a crown which she had long had in her pocket, with which she had intended to have bought play tickets.

It happened that the first person she saw in the poor widow's kitchen was the identical Mr. O'Neill. "I did not expect to see anybody here but you, Mrs. Smith," said Phoebe, blushing.

"So much the greater the pleasure of the meeting; to me, I mean, Miss Hill," said O'Neill, rising, and putting down a little boy, with whom he had been playing. Phoebe went on talking to the poor woman; and, after slipping the crown into her hand, said she would call again. O'Neill, surprised at the change in her manner, followed her when she left the house, and said, "It would be a great misfortune to me to have done anything to offend Miss Hill, especially if I could not conceive how or what it was, which is my case at this present speaking." And as the spruce glover spoke, he fixed his eyes upon Phoebe's ragged gloves. She drew them up in vain; and then said, with her natural simplicity and gentleness, "You have not done anything to offend me, Mr. O'Neill; but you are some way or other displeasing to my father and mother, and they have forbid me to wear the Limerick gloves."

"And sure Miss Hill would not be after changing her opinion of her humble servant for no reason in life but because her father and mother, who have taken a prejudice against him, are a little contrary."

"No," replied Phoebe; "I should not change my opinion without any reason; but I have not yet had time to fix my opinion of you, Mr. O'Neill."

"To let you know a piece of my mind, then, my dear Miss Hill," resumed he, "the more contrary they are, the more pride and joy it would give me to win and wear you, in spite of 'em all; and if without a farthing in your pocket, so much the more I should rejoice in the opportunity of proving to your dear self, and all else whom it may consarn, that Brian O'Neill is no fortune-hunter, and scorns them that are so narrow-minded as to think that no other kind of cattle but them there fortune-hunters can come out of all Ireland. So, my dear Phoebe, now we understand one another, I hope you will not be paining my eyes any longer with the sight of these odious brown bags, which are not fit to be worn by any Christian arms, to say nothing of Miss Hill's, which are the handsomest, without any compliment, that ever I saw, and, to my mind, would become a pair of Limerick gloves beyond anything: and I expect she'll show her generosity and proper spirit by putting them on immediately."

"You expect, sir!" repeated Miss Hill, with a look of more indignation than her gentle countenance had ever before been seen to assume. "Expect!" "If he had said hope," thought she, "it would have been another thing: but expect! what right has he to expect?"

Now Miss Hill, unfortunately, was not sufficiently acquainted with the Irish idiom to know that to expect, in Ireland, is the same thing as to hope in England; and, when her Irish admirer said "I expect," he meant only, in plain English, "I hope." But thus it is that a poor Irishman, often, for want of understanding the niceties of the English language, says the rudest when he means to say the civillest things imaginable.

Miss Hill's feelings were so much hurt by this unlucky "I expect" that the whole of his speech, which had before made some favourable impression upon her, now lost its effect: and she replied with proper spirit, as she thought, "You expect a great deal too much, Mr. O'Neill; and more than ever I gave you reason to do. It would be neither pleasure nor pride to me to be won and worn, as you were pleased to say, in spite of them all; and to be thrown, without a farthing in my pocket, upon the protection of one who expects so much at first setting out.—So I assure you, sir, whatever you may expect, I shall not put on the Limerick gloves."

Mr. O'Neill was not without his share of pride and proper spirit; nay, he had, it must be confessed, in common with some others of his countrymen, an improper share of pride and spirit. Fired by the lady's coldness, he poured forth a volley of reproaches; and ended by wishing, as he said, a good morning, for ever and ever, to one who could change her opinion, point blank, like the weathercock. "I am, miss, your most obedient; and I expect you'll never think no more of poor Brian O'Neill and the Limerick gloves."

If he had not been in too great a passion to observe anything, poor Brian O'Neill would have found out that Phoebe was not a weathercock: but he left her abruptly, and hurried away, imagining all the while that it was Phoebe, and not himself, who was in a rage. Thus, to the horseman who is galloping at full speed, the hedges, trees, and houses seem rapidly to recede, whilst, in reality, they never move from their places. It is he that flies from them, and not they from him.

On Monday morning Miss Jenny Brown, the perfumer's daughter, came to pay Phoebe a morning visit, with face of busy joy.

"So, my dear!" said she: "fine doings in Hereford! But what makes you look so downcast? To be sure you are invited, as well as the rest of us."

"Invited where?" cried Mrs. Hill, who was present, and who could never endure to hear of an invitation in which she was not included. "Invited where, pray, Miss Jenny?"

"La! have not you heard? Why, we all took it for granted that you and Miss Phoebe would have been the first and foremost to have been asked to Mr. O'Neill's ball."

"Ball!" cried Mrs. Hill; and luckily saved Phoebe, who was in some agitation, the trouble of speaking. "Why, this is a mighty sudden thing: I never heard a tittle of it before."

"Well, this is really extraordinary! And, Phoebe, have you not received a pair of Limerick gloves?"

"Yes, I have," said Phoebe, "but what then? What have my Limerick gloves to do with the ball?"

"A great deal," replied Jenny. "Don't you know that a pair of Limerick gloves is, as one may say, a ticket to this ball? for every lady that has been asked has had a pair sent to her along with the card; and I believe as many as twenty, besides myself, have been asked this morning."

Jenny then produced her new pair of Limerick gloves, and as she tried them on, and showed how well they fitted, she counted up the names of the ladies who, to her knowledge, were to be at this ball. When she had finished the catalogue, she expatiated upon the grand preparations which it was said the widow O'Neill, Mr. O'Neill's mother, was making for the supper, and concluded by condoling with Mrs. Hill for her misfortune in not having been invited. Jenny took her leave to get her dress in readiness: "for," added she, "Mr. O'Neill has engaged me to open the ball in case Phoebe does not go; but I suppose she will cheer up and go, as she has a pair of Limerick gloves as well as the rest of us."

There was a silence for some minutes after Jenny's departure, which was broken by Phoebe, who told her mother that, early in the morning, a note had been brought to her, which she had returned unopened, because she knew, from the handwriting of the direction, that it came from Mr. O'Neill.

We must observe that Phoebe had already told her mother of her meeting with this gentleman at the poor widow's, and of all that had passed between them afterwards. This openness on her part had softened the heart of Mrs. Hill, who was really inclined to be good-natured, provided people would allow that she had more penetration than any one else in Hereford. She was, moreover, a good deal piqued and alarmed by the idea that the perfumer's daughter might rival and outshine her own. Whilst she had thought herself sure of Mr. O'Neill's attachment to Phoebe, she had looked higher, especially as she was persuaded by the perfumer's lady to think that an Irishman could not but be a bad match; but now she began to suspect that the perfumer's lady had changed her opinion of Irishmen, since she did not object to her own Jenny's leading up the ball at Mr. O'Neill's.

All these thoughts passed rapidly in the mother's mind, and, with her fear of losing an admirer for her Phoebe, the value of that admirer suddenly rose in her estimation. Thus, at an auction, if a lot is going to be knocked down to a lady who is the only person that has bid for it, even she feels discontented, and despises that which nobody covets; but if, as the hammer is falling, many voices answer to the question, "Who bids more?" then her anxiety to secure the prize suddenly rises, and, rather than be outbid, she will give far beyond its value.

"Why, child," said Mrs. Hill, "since you have a pair of Limerick gloves; and since certainly that note was an invitation to us to this ball; and since it is much more fitting that you should open the ball than Jenny Brown; and since, after all, it was very handsome and genteel of the young man to say he would take you without a farthing in your pocket, which shows that those were misinformed who talked of him as an Irish adventurer; and since we are not certain 'twas he made away with the dog, although he said its barking was a great nuisance; there is no great reason to suppose he was the person who made the hole under the foundation of the cathedral, or that he could have such a wicked thought as to blow it up; and since he must be in a very good way of business to be able to afford giving away four or five guineas' worth of Limerick gloves, and balls and suppers; and since, after all, it is no fault of his to be an Irishman, I give it as my vote and opinion, my dear, that you put on your Limerick gloves and go to this ball; and I'll go and speak to your father, and bring him round to our opinion, and then I'll pay the morning visit I owe to the widow O'Neill and make up your quarrel with Brian. Love quarrels are easy to make up, you know, and then we shall have things all upon velvet again, and Jenny Brown need not come with her hypocritical condoling face to us any more."

After running this speech glibly off, Mrs. Hill, without waiting to hear a syllable from poor Phoebe, trotted off in search of her consort. It was not, however, quite so easy a task as his wife expected, to bring Mr. Hill round to her opinion. He was slow in declaring himself of any opinion; but when once he had said a thing, there was but little chance of altering his notions. On this occasion Mr. Hill was doubly bound to his prejudice against our unlucky Irishman; for he had mentioned with great solemnity at the club which he frequented the grand affair of the hole under the foundation of the cathedral, and his suspicions that there was a design to blow it up. Several of the club had laughed at this idea; others, who supposed that Mr. O'Neill was a Roman Catholic, and who had a confused notion that a Roman Catholic must be a very wicked, dangerous being, thought that there might be a great deal in the verger's suggestions, and observed that a very watchful eye ought to be kept upon this Irish glover, who had come to settle at Hereford nobody knew why, and who seemed to have money at command nobody knew how.

The news of this ball sounded to Mr. Hill's prejudiced imagination like the news of a conspiracy. "Ay! ay!" thought he; "the Irishman is cunning enough! But we shall be too many for him: he wants to throw all the good sober folks of Hereford off their guard by feasting, and dancing, and carousing, I take it, and so to perpetrate his evil design when it is least suspected; but we shall be prepared for him, fools as he takes us plain Englishmen to be, I warrant."

In consequence of these most shrewd cogitations, our verger silenced his wife with a peremptory nod when she came to persuade him to let Phoebe put on the Limerick gloves and go to the ball. "To this ball she shall not go, and I charge her not to put on those Limerick gloves as she values my blessing," said Mr. Hill. "Please to tell her so, Mrs. Hill, and trust to my judgment and discretion in all things, Mrs. Hill. Strange work may be in Hereford yet: but I'll say no more; I must go and consult with knowing men who are of my opinion."

He sallied forth, and Mrs. Hill was left in a state which only those who are troubled with the disease of excessive curiosity can rightly comprehend or compassionate. She hied her back to Phoebe, to whom she announced her father's answer, and then went gossiping to all her female acquaintance in Hereford, to tell them all that she knew, and all that she did not know, and to endeavour to find out a secret where there was none to be found.

There are trials of temper in all conditions, and no lady, in high or low life, could endure them with a better grace than Phoebe. Whilst Mr. and Mrs. Hill were busied abroad, there came to see Phoebe one of the widow Smith's children. With artless expressions of gratitude to Phoebe this little girl mixed the praises of O'Neill, who, she said, had been the constant friend of her mother, and had given her money every week since the fire happened. "Mammy loves him dearly for being so good-natured," continued the child; "and he has been good to other people as well as to us."

"To whom?" said Phoebe.

"To a poor man who has lodged for these few days past next door to us," replied the child; "I don't know his name rightly, but he is an Irishman, and he goes out a-haymaking in the daytime along with a number of others. He knew Mr. O'Neill in his own country, and he told mammy a great deal about his goodness."

As the child finished these words, Phoebe took out of a drawer some clothes, which she had made for the poor woman's children, and gave them to the little girl. It happened that the Limerick gloves had been thrown into this drawer; and Phoebe's favourable sentiments of the giver of those gloves were revived by what she had just heard, and by the confession Mrs. Hill had made, that she had no reasons, and but vague suspicious, for thinking ill of him. She laid the gloves perfectly smooth, and strewed over them, whilst the little girl went on talking of Mr. O'Neill, the leaves of a rose which she had worn on Sunday.

Mr. Hill was all this time in deep conference with those prudent men of Hereford who were of his own opinion, about the perilous hole under the cathedral. The ominous circumstance of this ball was also considered, the great expense at which the Irish glover lived, and his giving away gloves, which was a sure sign he was not under any necessity to sell them, and consequently a proof that, though he pretended to be a glover, he was something wrong in disguise. Upon putting all these things together, it was resolved by these over-wise politicians that the best thing that could be done for Hereford, and the only possible means of preventing the immediate destruction of its cathedral, would be to take Mr. O'Neill into custody. Upon recollection, however, it was perceived that there was no legal ground on which he could be attacked. At length, after consulting an attorney, they devised what they thought an admirable mode of proceeding.

Our Irish hero had not that punctuality which English tradesmen usually observe in the payment of bills; he had, the preceding year, run up a long bill with a grocer in Hereford, and, as he had not at Christmas cash in hand to pay it, he had given a note, payable six months after date. The grocer, at Mr. Hill's request, made over the note to him, and it was determined that the money should be demanded, as it was now due, and that, if it was not paid directly, O'Neill should be that night arrested. How Mr. Hill made the discovery of this debt to the grocer agree with his former notion that the Irish glover had always money at command we cannot well conceive, but anger and prejudice will swallow down the grossest contradictions without difficulty.

When Mr. Hill's clerk went to demand payment of the note, O'Neill's head was full of the ball which he was to give that evening. He was much surprised at the unexpected appearance of the note: he had not ready money by him to pay it; and after swearing a good deal at the clerk, and complaining of this ungenerous and ungentleman-like behaviour in the grocer and the tanner, he told the clerk to be gone, and not to be bothering him at such an unseasonable time: that he could not have the money then, and did not deserve to have it at all.

This language and conduct were rather new to the English clerk's mercantile ears: we cannot wonder that it should seem to him, as he said to his master, more the language of a madman than a man of business. This want of punctuality in money transactions, and this mode of treating contracts as matters of favour and affection, might not have damned the fame of our hero in his own country, where such conduct is, alas! too common; but he was now in a kingdom where the manners and customs are so directly opposite, that he could meet with no allowance for his national faults. It would be well for his countrymen if they were made, even by a few mortifications, somewhat sensible of this important difference in the habits of Irish and English traders before they come to settle in England.

But to proceed with our story. On the night of Mr. O'Neill's grand ball, as he was seeing his fair partner, the perfumer's daughter, safe home, he felt himself tapped on the shoulder by no friendly hand. When he was told that he was the king's prisoner, he vociferated with sundry strange oaths, which we forbear to repeat. "No, I am not the king's prisoner! I am the prisoner of that shabby, rascally tanner, Jonathan Hill. None but he would arrest a gentleman in this way, for a trifle not worth mentioning."

Miss Jenny Brown screamed when she found herself under the protection of a man who was arrested; and, what between her screams and his oaths, there was such a disturbance that a mob gathered.

Among this mob there was a party of Irish haymakers, who, after returning late from a hard day's work, had been drinking in a neighbouring ale-house. With one accord they took part with their countryman, and would have rescued him from the civil officers with all the pleasure in life if he had not fortunately possessed just sufficient sense and command of himself to restrain their party spirit, and to forbid them, as they valued his life and reputation, to interfere, by word or deed, in his defence.

He then despatched one of the haymakers home to his mother, to inform her of what had happened, and to request that she would get somebody to be bail for him as soon as possible, as the officers said they could not let him out of their sight till he was bailed by substantial people, or till the debt was discharged.

The widow O'Neill was just putting out the candles in the ball-room when this news of her son's arrest was brought to her. We pass over Hibernian exclamations: she consoled her pride by reflecting that it would certainly be the most easy thing imaginable to procure bail for Mr. O'Neill in Hereford, where he had so many friends who had just been dancing at his house; but to dance at his house she found was one thing and to be bail for him quite another. Each guest sent excuses, and the widow O'Neill was astonished at what never fails to astonish everybody when it happens to themselves. "Rather than let my son be detained in this manner for a paltry debt," cried she, "I'd sell all I have within half an hour to a pawnbroker." It was well no pawnbroker heard this declaration: she was too warm to consider economy. She sent for a pawnbroker, who lived in the same street, and, after pledging goods to treble the amount of the debt, she obtained ready money for her son's release.

O'Neill, after being in custody for about an hour and a half, was set at liberty upon the payment of his debt. As he passed by the cathedral in his way home, he heard the clock strike; and he called to a man, who was walking backwards and forwards in the churchyard, to ask whether it was two or three that the clock struck. "Three," answered the man; "and, as yet, all is safe."

O'Neill, whose head was full of other things, did not stop to inquire the meaning of these last words. He little suspected that this man was a watchman whom the over-vigilant verger had stationed there to guard the Hereford Cathedral from his attacks. O'Neill little guessed that he had been arrested merely to keep him from blowing up the cathedral this night. The arrest had an excellent effect upon his mind, for he was a young man of good sense: it made him resolve to retrench his expenses in time, to live

"Indeed, Mr. Verger! And pray how, and by whom, was the cathedral to be blown up? and what was there diabolical in this ball?"

Here Mr. Hill let Mr. Marshal into the whole history of his early dislike to O'Neill, and his shrewd suspicions of him the first moment he saw him in Hereford: related in the most prolix manner all that the reader knows already, and concluded by saying that, as he was now certain of his facts, he was come to swear examinations against this villanous Irishman, who, he hoped, would be speedily brought to justice, as he deserved.

"To justice he shall be brought, as he deserves," said Mr. Marshal; "but before I write, and before you swear, will you have the goodness to inform me how you have made yourself as certain, as you evidently are, of what you call your facts?"

"Sir, that is a secret," replied our wise man, "which I shall trust to you alone;" and he whispered into Mr. Marshal's ear that, his information came from Bampfylde the Second, king of the gipsies.

Mr. Marshal instantly burst into laughter; then composing himself, said: "My good sir, I am really glad that you have proceeded no farther in this business; and that no one in Hereford, beside myself, knows that you were on the point of swearing examinations against a man on the evidence of Bampfylde the Second, king of the gipsies. My dear sir, it would be a standing joke against you to the end of your days. A grave man like Mr. Hill! and a verger too! Why you would be the laughing-stock of Hereford!"

Now Mr. Marshal well knew the character of the man to whom he was talking, who, above all things on earth, dreaded to be laughed at. Mr. Hill coloured all over his face, and, pushing back his wig by way of settling it, showed that he blushed not only all over his face, but all over his head.

"Why, Mr. Marshal, sir," said he, "as to my being laughed at, it is what I did not look for, being, as there are, some men in Hereford to whom I have mentioned that hole in the cathedral, who have thought it no laughing matter, and who have been precisely of my own opinion thereupon."

"But did you tell these gentlemen that you had been consulting the king of the gipsies?"

"No, sir, no: I can't say that I did."

"Then I advise you, keep your own counsel, as I will."

Mr. Hill, whose imagination wavered between the hole in the cathedral and his rick of bark on one side, and between his rick of bark and his dog Jowler on the other, now began to talk of the dog, and now of the rick of bark; and when he had exhausted all he had to say upon these subjects, Mr. Marshal gently pulled him towards the window, and putting a spy-glass into his hand, bade him look towards his own tan-yard, and tell him what he saw. To his great surprise, Mr. Hill saw his rick of bark re-built. "Why, it was not there last night," exclaimed he, rubbing his eyes. "Why, some conjuror must have done this."

"No," replied Mr. Marshal, "no conjuror did it: but your friend Bampfylde the Second, king of the gipsies, was the cause of its being re-built; and here is the man who actually pulled it down, and who actually re-built it."

As he said these words Mr. Marshal opened the door of an adjoining room and beckoned to the Irish haymaker, who had been taken into custody about an hour before this time. The watch who took Paddy had called at Mr. Hill's house to tell him what had happened, but Mr. Hill was not then at home.

It was with much surprise that the verger heard the simple truth from this poor fellow; but no sooner was he convinced that O'Neill was innocent as to this affair, than he recurred to his other ground of suspicion, the loss of his dog.

The Irish haymaker now stepped forward, and, with a peculiar twist of the hips and shoulders, which those only who have seen it can picture to themselves, said, "Plase your honour's honour, I have a little word to say too about the dog."

"Say it, then," said Mr. Marshal.

"Plase your honour, if I might expect to be forgiven, and let off for pulling down the jontleman's stack, I might be able to tell him what I know about the dog."

"If you can tell me anything about my dog," said the tanner, "I will freely forgive you for pulling down the rick: especially as you have built it up again. Speak the truth, now: did not O'Neill make away with the dog?"

"Not at all, at all, plase your honour," replied the haymaker: "and the truth of the matter is, I know nothing of the dog, good or bad; but I know something of his collar, if your name, plase your honour, is Hill, as I take it to be."

"My name is Hill: proceed," said the tanner, with great eagerness. "You know something about the collar of my dog Jowler?"

"Plase your honour, this much I know, any way, that it is now, or was the night before last, at the pawnbroker's there, below in town; for, plase your honour, I was sent late at night (that night that Mr. O'Neill, long life to him! was arrested) to the pawnbroker's for a Jew by Mrs. O'Neill, poor creature! She was in great trouble that same time."

"Very likely," interrupted Mr. Hill: "but go on to the collar; what of the collar?"

"She sent me—I'll tell you the story, plase your honour, out of the face—she sent me to the pawnbroker's for the Jew; and, it being so late at night, the shop was shut, and it was with all the trouble in life that I got into the house any way: and, when I got in, there was none but a slip of a boy up; and he set down the light that he had in his hand, and ran up the stairs to waken his master: and, whilst he was gone, I just made bold to look round at what sort of a place I was in, and at the old clothes and rags and scraps; there was a sort of a frieze trusty."

"A trusty!" said Mr. Hill; "what is that, pray?"

"A big coat, sure, plase your honour: there was a frieze big coat lying in a corner, which I had my eye upon, to trate myself to: I having, as I then thought, money in my little purse enough for it. Well, I won't trouble your honour's honour with telling of you now how I lost my purse in the field, as I found after; but about the big coat—as I was saying, I just lifted it off the ground to see would it fit me; and, as I swung it round, something, plase your honour, hit me a great knock on the shins: it was in the pocket of the coat, whatever it was, I knew; so I looks into the pocket to see what was it, plase your honour, and out I pulls a hammer and a dog-collar: it was a wonder, both together, they did not break my shins entirely: but it's no matter for my shins now; so, before the boy came down, I just out of idleness spelt out to myself the name that was upon the collar: there were two names, plase your honour, and out of the first there were so many letters hammered out I could make nothing of it at all, at all; but the other name was plain enough to read, any way, and it was Hill, plase your honour's honour, as sure as life: Hill, now."

This story was related in tones and gestures which were so new and strange to English ears and eyes, that even the solemnity of our verger gave way to laughter.

Mr. Marshal sent a summons for the pawnbroker, that he might learn from him how he came by the dog-collar. The pawnbroker, when he found from Mr. Marshal that he could by no other means save himself from being committed to prison, confessed that the collar had been sold to him by Bampfylde the Second, king of the gipsies.

A warrant was immediately despatched for his majesty; and Mr. Hill was a good deal alarmed by the fear of its being known in Hereford that he was on the point of swearing examinations against an innocent man upon the evidence of a dog-stealer and a gipsy.

Bampfylde the Second made no sublime appearance when he was brought before Mr. Marshal, nor could all his astrology avail upon this occasion. The evidence of the pawnbroker was so positive as to the fact of his having sold to him the dog-collar, that there was no resource left for Bampfylde but an appeal to Mr. Hill's mercy. He fell on his knees, and confessed that it was he who stole the dog, which used to bark at him at night so furiously, that he could not commit certain petty depredations by which, as much as by telling fortunes, he made his livelihood.

"And so," said Mr. Marshal, with a sternness of manner which till now he had never shown, "to screen yourself, you accused an innocent man; and by your vile arts would have driven him from Hereford, and have set two families for ever at variance, to conceal that you had stolen a dog."

The king of the gipsies was, without further ceremony, committed to the house of correction. We should not omit to mention that, on searching his hat, the Irish haymaker's purse was found, which some of his majesty's train had emptied. The whole set of gipsies decamped upon the news of the apprehension of their monarch.

Mr. Hill stood in profound silence, leaning upon his walking-stick, whilst the committal was making out for Bampfylde the Second. The fear of ridicule was struggling with the natural positiveness of his temper. He was dreadfully afraid that the story of his being taken in by the king of the gipsies would get abroad; and, at the same time, he was unwilling to give up his prejudice against the Irish glover.

"But, Mr. Marshal," cried he, after a long silence, "the hole under the foundation of the cathedral has never been accounted for—that is, was, and ever will be, an ugly mystery to me; and I never can have a good opinion of this Irishman till it is cleared up, nor can I think the cathedral in safety."

"What!" said Mr. Marshal, with an arch smile, "I suppose the verses of the oracle still work upon your imagination, Mr. Hill. They are excellent in their kind. I must have them by heart, that when I am asked the reason why Mr. Hill has taken an aversion to an Irish glover, I may be able to repeat them:—

"Now, take my word,
Wise men of Hereford,
None in safety may be,
Till the bad man doth flee."

"You'll oblige me, sir," said the verger, "if you would never repeat those verses, sir, nor mention, in any company, the affair of the king of the gipsies."

"I will oblige you," replied Mr. Marshal, "if you will oblige me. Will you tell me honestly whether, now that you find this Mr. O'Neill is neither a dog-killer nor a puller-down of bark-ricks, you feel that you could forgive him for being an Irishman, if the mystery, as you call it, of the hole under the cathedral was cleared up?"

"But that is not cleared up, I say, sir," cried Mr. Hill, striking his walking-stick forcibly upon the ground with both his hands. "As to the matter of his being an Irishman, I have nothing to say to it; I am not saying anything about that, for I know we all are born where it pleases God, and an Irishman may be as good as another. I know that much, Mr. Marshal, and I am not one of those illiberal-minded, ignorant people that cannot abide a man that was not born in England. Ireland is now in his majesty's dominions. I know very well, Mr. Marshal; and I have no manner of doubt, as I said before, that an Irishman born may be as good, almost, as an Englishman born."

"I am glad," said Mr. Marshal, "to hear you speak—almost as reasonably as an Englishman born and every man ought to speak; and I am convinced that you have too much English hospitality to persecute an inoffensive stranger, who comes amongst us trusting to our justice and good nature."

"I would not persecute a stranger, God forbid!" replied the verger, "if he was, as you say, inoffensive."

"And if he was not only inoffensive, but ready to do every service in his power to those who are in want of his assistance, we should not return evil for good, should we?"

"That would be uncharitable, to be sure; and, moreover, a scandal," said the verger.

"Then," said Mr. Marshal, "will you walk with me as far as the Widow Smith's, the poor woman whose house was burnt last winter? This haymaker, who lodged near her, can show us the way to her present abode."

During his examination of Paddy M'Cormack, who would tell his whole history, as he called it, out of the face, Mr. Marshal heard several instances of the humanity and goodness of O'Neill, which Paddy related to excuse himself for that warmth of attachment to his cause that had been manifested so injudiciously by pulling down the rick of bark in revenge for the rest. Amongst other things, Paddy mentioned his countryman's goodness to the Widow Smith. Mr. Marshal was determined, therefore, to see whether he had, in this instance, spoken the truth; and he took Hill with him, in hopes of being able to show him the favourable side of O'Neill's character.

Things turned out just as Mr. Marshal expected. The poor widow and her family, in the most simple and affecting manner, described the distress from which they had been relieved by the good gentleman; and lady—the lady was Phoebe Hill; and the praises that were bestowed upon Phoebe were delightful to her father's ear, whose angry passions had now all subsided.

The benevolent Mr. Marshal seized the moment when he saw Mr. Hill's heart was touched, and exclaimed, "I must be acquainted with this Mr. O'Neill. I am sure we people of Hereford ought to show some hospitality to a stranger who has so much humanity. Mr. Hill, will you dine with him to- morrow at my house?"

Mr. Hill was just going to accept of this invitation, when the recollection of all he had said to his club about the hole under the cathedral came across him, and, drawing Mr. Marshal aside, he whispered, "But, sir, sir, that affair of the hole under the cathedral has not been cleared up yet."

At this instant the Widow Smith exclaimed, "Oh! here comes my little Mary" (one of her children, who came running in); "this is the little girl, sir, to whom the lady has been so good. Make your curtsey, child. Where have you been all this while?"

"Mammy," said the child, "I've been showing the lady my rat."

"Lord bless her! Gentlemen, the child has been wanting me this many a day to go to see this tame rat of hers; but I could never get time, never—and I wondered, too, at the child's liking such a creature. Tell the gentlemen, dear, about your rat. All I know is that, let her have but never such a tiny bit of bread for breakfast or supper, she saves a little of that little for this rat of hers; she and her brothers have found it out somewhere by the cathedral."

"It comes out of a hole under the wall of the cathedral," said one of the older boys; "and we have diverted ourselves watching it, and sometimes we have put victuals for it—so it has grown, in a manner, tame-like."

Mr. Hill and Mr. Marshal looked at one another during this speech; and the dread of ridicule again seized on Mr. Hill, when he apprehended that, after all he had said, the mountain might at last bring forth—a rat. Mr. Marshal, who instantly saw what passed in the verger's mind, relieved him from this fear by refraining even from a smile on this occasion. He only said to the child, in a grave manner, "I am afraid, my dear, we shall be obliged to spoil your diversion. Mr. Verger, here, cannot suffer rat- holes in the cathedral; but, to make you amends for the loss of your favourite, I will give you a very pretty little dog, if you have a mind."

The child was well pleased with this promise; and, at Mr. Marshal's desire, she then went along with him and Mr. Hill to the cathedral, and they placed themselves at a little distance from that hole which had created so much disturbance. The child soon brought the dreadful enemy to light; and Mr. Hill, with a faint laugh, said, "I'm glad it's no worse, but there were many in our club who were of my opinion; and, if they had not suspected O'Neill too, I am sure I should never have given you so much trouble, sir, as I have done this morning. But I hope, as the club know nothing about that vagabond, that king of the gipsies, you will not let any one know anything about the prophecy, and all that? I am sure I am very sorry to have given you so much trouble, Mr. Marshal."

Mr. Marshal assured him that he did not regret the time which he had spent in endeavouring to clear up all those mysteries and suspicions; and Mr. Hill gladly accepted his invitation to meet O'Neill at his house the next day. No sooner had Mr. Marshal brought one of the parties to reason and good humour than he went to prepare the other for a reconciliation. O'Neill and his mother were both people of warm but forgiving tempers—the arrest was fresh in their minds; but when Mr. Marshal represented to them the whole affair, and the verger's prejudices, in a humorous light, they joined in the good-natured laugh; and O'Neill declared that, for his part, he was ready to forgive and to forget everything if he could but see Miss Phoebe in the Limerick gloves.

Phoebe appeared the next day, at Mr. Marshal's, in the Limerick gloves; and no perfume ever was so delightful to her lover as the smell of the rose-leaves in which they had been kept.

Mr. Marshal had the benevolent pleasure of reconciling the two families. The tanner and the glover of Hereford became, from bitter enemies, useful friends to each other; and they were convinced by experience that nothing could be more for their mutual advantage than to live in union.

MADAME DE FLEURY

CHAPTER I

"There oft are heard the notes of infant woe,
The short thick sob, loud scream, and shriller squall—
How can you, mothers, vex your infants so?"
—POPE

"D'abord, madame, c'est impossible!—Madame ne descendra pas ici?" said Francois, the footman of Madame de Fleury, with a half expostulatory, half indignant look, as he let down the step of her carriage at the entrance of a dirty passage, that led to one of the most miserable-looking houses in Paris.

"But what can be the cause of the cries which I hear in this house?" said Madame de Fleury.

"'Tis only some child who is crying," replied Francois; and he would have put up the step, but his lady was not satisfied.

"'Tis nothing in the world," continued he, with a look of appeal to the coachman, "it can be nothing, but some children who are locked up there above. The mother, the workwoman my lady wants, is not at home: that's certain."

"I must know the cause of these cries; I must see these children" said Madame de Fleury, getting out of her carriage.

Francois held his arm for his lady as she got out.

"Bon!" cried he, with an air of vexation. "Si madame la vent absolument, a la bonne heure!—Mais madame sera abimee. Madame verra que j'ai raison. Madame ne montera jamais ce vilain escalier. D'ailleurs c'est au cinquieme. Mais, madame, c'est impossible."

Notwithstanding the impossibility, Madame de Fleury proceeded; and bidding her talkative footman wait in the entry, made her way up the dark, dirty, broken staircase, the sound of the cries increasing every instant, till, as she reached the fifth storey, she heard the shrieks of one in violent pain. She hastened to the door of the room from which the cries proceeded; the door was fastened, and the noise was so great that, though she knocked as loud as she was able, she could not immediately make herself heard. At last the voice of a child from within answered, "The door is locked—mamma has the key in her pocket, and won't be home till night; and here's Victoire has tumbled from the top of the big press, and it is she that is shrieking so."

Madame de Fleury ran down the stairs which she had ascended with so much difficulty, called to her footman, who was waiting in the entry, despatched him for a surgeon, and then she returned to obtain from some people who lodged in the house assistance to force open the door of the room in which the children were confined.

On the next floor there was a smith at work, filing so earnestly that he did not hear the screams of the children. When his door was pushed open, and the bright vision of Madame de Fleury appeared to him, his astonishment was so great that he seemed incapable of comprehending what she said. In a strong provincial accent he repeated, "Plait-il?" and stood aghast till she had explained herself three times; then suddenly exclaiming, "Ah! c'est ca;"—he collected his tools precipitately, and followed to obey her orders. The door of the room was at last forced half open, for a press that had been overturned prevented its opening entirely. The horrible smells that issued did not overcome Madame de Fleury's humanity: she squeezed her way into the room, and behind the fallen press saw three little children: the youngest, almost an infant, ceased roaring, and ran to a corner; the eldest, a boy of about eight years old, whose face and clothes were covered with blood, held on his knee a girl younger than himself, whom he was trying to pacify, but who struggled most violently and screamed incessantly, regardless of Madame de Fleury, to whose questions she made no answer.

"Where are you hurt, my dear?" repeated Madame de Fleury in a soothing voice. "Only tell me where you feel pain?"

The boy, showing his sister's arm, said, in a surly tone—"It is this that is hurt—but it was not I did it."

"It was, it was!" cried the girl as loud as she could vociferate: "it was Maurice threw me down from the top of the press."

"No—it was you that were pushing me, Victoire, and you fell backwards.—Have done screeching, and show your arm to the lady."

"I can't," said the girl.

"She won't," said the boy.

"She cannot," said Madame de Fleury, kneeling down to examine it. "She cannot move it; I am afraid that it is broken."

"Don't touch it! don't touch it!" cried the girl, screaming more violently.

"Ma'am, she screams that way for nothing often," said the boy. "Her arm is no more broke than mine, I'm sure; she'll move it well enough when she's not cross."

"I am afraid," said Madame de Fleury, "that her arm is broken."

"Is it indeed?" said the boy, with a look of terror.

"Oh! don't touch it—you'll kill me; you are killing me," screamed the poor girl, whilst Madame de Fleury with the greatest care endeavoured to join the bones in their proper place, and resolved to hold the arm till the arrival of the surgeon.

From the feminine appearance of this lady, no stranger would have expected such resolution; but with all the natural sensibility and graceful delicacy of her sex, she had none of that weakness or affection which incapacitates from being useful in real distress. In most sudden accidents, and in all domestic misfortunes, female resolution and presence of mind are indispensably requisite: safety, health, and life often depend upon the fortitude of women. Happy they who, like Madame de Fleury, possess strength of mind united with the utmost gentleness of manner and tenderness of disposition!

Soothed by this lady's sweet voice, the child's rage subsided; and no longer struggling, the poor little girl sat quietly on her lap, sometimes writhing and moaning with pain.

The surgeon at length arrived: her arm was set: and he said "that she had probably been saved much future pain by Madame de Fleury's presence of mind."

"Sir,—will it soon be well?" said Maurice to the surgeon.

"Oh yes, very soon, I dare say," said the little girl. "To-morrow, perhaps; for now that it is tied up it does not hurt me to signify—and after all, I do believe, Maurice, it was not you threw me down."

As she spoke, she held up her face to kiss her brother.—"That is right," said Madame de Fleury; "there is a good sister."

The little girl put out her lips, offering a second kiss, but the boy turned hastily away to rub the tears from his eyes with the back of his hand.

"I am not cross now: am I, Maurice?"

"No, Victoire; I was cross myself when I said that."

As Victoire was going to speak again, the surgeon imposed silence, observing that she must be put to bed, and should be kept quiet. Madame de Fleury laid her upon the bed, as soon as Maurice had cleared it of the things with which it was covered; and as they were spreading the ragged blanket over the little girl, she whispered a request to Madame de Fleury that she would "stay till her mamma came home, to beg Maurice off from being whipped, if mamma should be angry."

Touched by this instance of goodness, and compassionating the desolate condition of these children, Madame de Fleury complied with Victoire's request; resolving to remonstrate with their mother for leaving them locked up in this manner. They did not know to what part of the town their mother was gone; they could tell only "that she was to go to a great many different places to carry back work, and to bring home more, and that she expected to be in by five." It was now half after four.

Whilst Madame de Fleury waited, she asked the boy to give her a full account of the manner in which the accident had happened.

"Why, ma'am," said Maurice, twisting and untwisting a ragged handkerchief as he spoke, "the first beginning of all the mischief was, we had nothing to do, so we went to the ashes to make dirt pies; but Babet would go so close that she burnt her petticoat, and threw about all our ashes, and plagued us, and we whipped her. But all would not do, she would not be quiet; so to get out of her reach, we climbed up by this chair on the table to the top of the press, and there we were well enough for a little while, till somehow we began to quarrel about the old scissors, and we struggled hard for them till I got this cut."

Here he unwound the handkerchief, and for the first time showed the wound, which he had never mentioned before.

"Then," continued he, "when I got the cut, I shoved Victoire, and she pushed at me again, and I was keeping her off, and her foot slipped, and down she fell, and caught by the press-door, and pulled it and me after her, and that's all I know."

"It is well that you were not both killed," said Madame de Fleury. "Are you often left locked up in this manner by yourselves, and without anything to do?"

"Yes, always, when mamma is abroad, except sometimes we are let out upon the stairs or in the street; but mamma says we get into mischief there."

This dialogue was interrupted by the return of the mother. She came upstairs slowly, much fatigued, and with a heavy bundle under her arm.

"How now! Maurice, how comes my door open? What's all this?" cried she, in an angry voice; but seeing a lady sitting upon her child's bed, she stopped short in great astonishment. Madame de Fleury related what had happened, and averted her anger from Maurice by gently expostulating upon the hardship and hazard of leaving her young children in this manner during so many hours of the day.

"Why, my lady," replied the poor woman, wiping her forehead, "every hard- working woman in Paris does the same with her children; and what can I do else? I must earn bread for these helpless ones, and to do that I must be out backwards and forwards, and to the furthest parts of the town, often from morning till night, with those that employ me; and I cannot afford to send the children to school, or to keep any kind of a servant to look after them; and when I'm away, if I let them run about these stairs and entries, or go into the sheets, they do get a little exercise and air, to be sure, such as it is on which account I do let them out sometimes; but then a deal of mischief comes of that, too: they learn all kinds of wickedness, and would grow up to be no better than pickpockets, if they were let often to consort with the little vagabonds they find in the streets. So what to do better for them I don't know."

The poor mother sat down upon the fallen press, looked at Victoire, and wept bitterly. Madame de Fleury was struck with compassion; but she did not satisfy her feelings merely by words or comfort or by the easy donation of some money—she resolved to do something more, and something better.

CHAPTER II

"Come often, then; for haply in my bower
Amusement, knowledge, wisdom, thou may'st gain:
If I one soul improve, I have not lived in vain."
—BEATTIE.

It is not so easy to do good as those who have never attempted it may imagine; and they who without consideration follow the mere instinct of pity, often by their imprudent generosity create evils more pernicious to society than any which they partially remedy. "Warm Charity, the general friend," may become the general enemy, unless she consults her head as well as her heart. Whilst she pleases herself with the idea that she daily feeds hundreds of the poor, she is perhaps preparing want and famine for thousands. Whilst she delights herself with the anticipation of gratitude for her bounties, she is often exciting only unreasonable expectations, inducing habits of dependence and submission to slavery.

Those who wish to do good should attend to experience, from whom they may receive lessons upon the largest scale that time and numbers can afford.

Madame de Fleury was aware that neither a benevolent disposition nor a large fortune were sufficient to enable her to be of real service, without the constant exercise of her judgment. She had, therefore, listened with deference to the conversation of well-informed men upon those subjects on which ladies have not always the means or the wish to acquire extensive and accurate knowledge. Though a Parisian belle, she had read with attention some of those books which are generally thought too dry or too deep for her sex. Consequently, her benevolence was neither wild in theory nor precipitate nor ostentatious in practice.

Touched with compassion for a little girl whose arm had been accidentally broken, and shocked by the discovery of the confinement and the dangers to which numbers of children in Paris were doomed, she did not make a parade of her sensibility. She did not talk of her feelings in fine sentences to a circle of opulent admirers, nor did she project for the relief of the little sufferers some magnificent establishment which she could not execute or superintend. She was contented with attempting only what she had reasonable hopes of accomplishing.

The gift of education she believed to be more advantageous than the gift of money to the poor, as it ensures the means both of future subsistence and happiness. But the application even of this incontrovertible principle requires caution and judgment. To crowd numbers of children into a place called a school, to abandon them to the management of any person called a schoolmaster or a schoolmistress, is not sufficient to secure the blessings of a good education. Madame de Fleury was sensible that the greatest care is necessary in the choice of the person to whom young children are to be entrusted; she knew that only a certain number can be properly directed by one superintendent, and that, by attempting to do too much, she might do nothing, or worse than nothing. Her school was formed, therefore, on a small scale, which she could enlarge to any extent, if it should be found to succeed. From some of the families of poor people, who, in earning their bread, are obliged to spend most of the day from home, she selected twelve little girls, of whom Victoire was the eldest, and she was between six and seven.

The person under whose care Madame de Fleury wished to place these children was a nun of the Soeurs de la Charite, with whose simplicity of character, benevolence, and mild, steady temper she was thoroughly acquainted. Sister Frances was delighted with the plan. Any scheme that promised to be of service to her follow-creatures was sure of meeting with her approbation; but this suited her taste peculiarly, because she was extremely fond of children. No young person had ever boarded six months at her convent without becoming attached to good Sister Frances.

The period of which we are writing was some years before convents were abolished; but the strictness of their rules had in many instances been considerably relaxed. Without much difficulty, permission was obtained from the abbess for our nun to devote her time during the day to the care of these poor children, upon condition that she should regularly return to her convent every night before evening prayers. The house which Madame de Fleury chose for her little school was in an airy part of the town; it did not face the street, but was separated from other buildings at the back of a court, retired from noise and bustle. The two rooms intended for the occupation of the children were neat and clean, but perfectly simple, with whitewashed walls, furnished only with wooden stools and benches, and plain deal tables. The kitchen was well lighted (for light is essential to cleanliness), and it was provided with utensils; and for these appropriate places were allotted, to give the habit and the taste of order. The schoolroom opened into a garden larger than is usually seen in towns. The nun, who had been accustomed to purchase provisions for her convent, undertook to prepare daily for the children breakfast and dinner; they were to sup and sleep at their respective homes. Their parents were to take them to Sister Frances every morning when they went out to work, and to call for them upon their return home every evening. By this arrangement, the natural ties of affection and intimacy between the children and their parents would not be loosened; they would be separate only at the time when their absence must be inevitable. Madame de Fleury thought that any education which estranges children entirely from their parents must be fundamentally erroneous; that such a separation must tend to destroy that sense of filial affection and duty, and those principles of domestic subordination, on which so many of the interests and much of the virtue and happiness of society depend. The parents of these poor children were eager to trust them to her care, and they strenuously endeavoured to promote what they perceived to be entirely to their advantage. They promised to take their daughters to school punctually every morning—a promise which was likely to be kept, as a good breakfast was to be ready at a certain hour, and not to wait for anybody. The parents looked forward with pleasure, also, to the idea of calling for their little girls at the end of their day's labour, and of taking them home to their family supper. During the intermediate hours the children were constantly to be employed, or in exercise. It was difficult to provide suitable employments for their early age; but even the youngest of those admitted could be taught to wind balls of cotton, thread, and silk for haberdashers; or they could shell peas and beans, &c., for a neighbouring traiteur; or they could weed in a garden. The next in age could learn knitting and plain work, reading, writing, and arithmetic. As the girls should grow up, they were to be made useful in the care of the house. Sister Frances said she could teach them to wash and iron, and that she would make them as skilful in cookery as she was herself. This last was doubtless a rash promise; for in most of the mysteries of the culinary art, especially in the medical branches of it, in making savoury messes palatable to the sick, few could hope to equal the neat-handed Sister Frances. She had a variety of other accomplishments; but her humility and good sense forbade her upon the present occasion to mention these. She said nothing of embroidery, or of painting, or of cutting out paper, or of carving in ivory, though in all these she excelled: her cuttings- out in paper were exquisite as the finest lace; her embroidered housewives, and her painted boxes, and her fan-mounts, and her curiously- wrought ivory toys, had obtained for her the highest reputation in the convent amongst the best judges in the world. Those only who have philosophically studied and thoroughly understand the nature of fame and vanity can justly appreciate the self-denial or magnanimity of Sister Frances, in forbearing to enumerate or boast of these things. She alluded to them but once, and in the slightest and most humble manner.

"These little creatures are too young for us to think of teaching them anything but plain work at present; but if hereafter any of them should show a superior genius we can cultivate it properly. Heaven has been pleased to endow me with the means—at least, our convent says so."

The actions of Sister Frances showed as much moderation as her words; for though she was strongly tempted to adorn her new dwelling with those specimens of her skill which had long been the glory of her apartment in the convent, yet she resisted the impulse, and contented herself with hanging over the chimney-piece of her schoolroom a Madonna of her own painting.

The day arrived when she was to receive her pupils in their new habitation. When the children entered the room for the first time, they paid the Madonna the homage of their unfeigned admiration. Involuntarily the little crowd stopped short at the sight of the picture. Some dormant emotions of human vanity were now awakened—played for a moment about the heart of Sister Frances—and may be forgiven. Her vanity was innocent and transient, her benevolence permanent and useful. Repressing the vain- glory of an artist, as she fixed her eyes upon the Madonna, her thoughts rose to higher objects, and she seized this happy moment to impress upon the minds of her young pupils their first religious ideas and feelings. There was such unaffected piety in her manner, such goodness in her countenance, such persuasion in her voice, and simplicity in her words, that the impression she made was at once serious, pleasing, and not to be effaced. Much depends upon the moment and the manner in which the first notions of religion are communicated to children; if these ideas be connected with terror, and produced when the mind is sullen or in a state of dejection, the future religious feelings are sometimes of a gloomy, dispiriting sort; but if the first impression be made when the heart is expanded by hope or touched by affection, these emotions are happily and permanently associated with religion. This should be particularly attended to by those who undertake the instruction of the children of the poor, who must lead a life of labour, and can seldom have leisure or inclination, when arrived at years of discretion, to re-examine the principles early infused into their minds. They cannot in their riper age conquer by reason those superstitions terrors, or bigoted prejudices, which render their victims miserable, or perhaps criminal. To attempt to rectify any errors in the foundation after an edifice has been constructed is dangerous: the foundation, therefore, should be laid with care. The religious opinions of Sister Frances were strictly united with just rules of morality, strongly enforcing, as the essential means of obtaining present and future happiness, the practice of the social virtues, so that no good or wise persons, however they might differ from her in modes of faith, could doubt the beneficial influence of her general principles, or disapprove of the manner in which they were inculcated.

Detached from every other worldly interest, this benevolent nun devoted all her earthly thoughts to the children of whom she had undertaken the charge. She watched over them with unceasing vigilance, whilst diffidence of her own abilities was happily supported by her high opinion of Madame de Fleury's judgment. This lady constantly visited her pupils every week; not in the hasty, negligent manner in which fine ladies sometimes visit charitable institutions, imagining that the honour of their presence is to work miracles, and that everything will go on rightly when they have said, "Let it be so," or, "I must have it so." Madame de Fleury's visits were not of this dictatorial or cursory nature. Not minutes, but hours, she devoted to these children—she who could charm by the grace of her manners, and delight by the elegance of her conversation, the most polished circles and the best-informed societies of Paris, preferred to the glory of being admired the pleasure of being useful:—

"Her life, as lovely as her face,
Each duty mark'd with every grace;
Her native sense improved by reading,
Her native sweetness by good breeding."

CHAPTER III

*"Ah me! how much I fear lest pride it be;
But if that pride it be which thus inspires,
Beware, ye dames! with nice discernment see
Ye quench not too the sparks of nobler fires."*
—SHENSTONE.

By repeated observation, and by attending to the minute reports of Sister Frances, Madame de Fleury soon became acquainted with the habits and temper of each individual in this little society. The most intelligent and the most amiable of these children was Victoire. Whence her superiority arose, whether her abilities were naturally more vivacious than those of her companions, or whether they had been more early developed by accidental excitation, we cannot pretend to determine, lest we should involve ourselves in the intricate question respecting natural genius—a metaphysical point, which we shall not in this place stop to discuss. Till the world has an accurate philosophical dictionary (a work not to be expected in less than half a dozen centuries), this question will never be decided to general satisfaction. In the meantime we may proceed with our story.

Deep was the impression made on Victoire's heart by the kindness that Madame de Fleury showed her at the time her arm was broken; and her gratitude was expressed with all the enthusiastic fondness of childhood. Whenever she spoke or heard of Madame de Fleury her countenance became interested and animated in a degree that would have astonished a cool English spectator. Every morning her first question to Sister Frances was: "Will she come to-day?" If Madame de Fleury was expected, the hours and the minutes were counted, and the sand in the hour-glass that stood on the schoolroom table was frequently shaken. The moment she appeared Victoire ran to her, and was silent; satisfied with standing close beside her, holding her gown when unperceived, and watching, as she spoke and moved, every turn of her countenance. Delighted by these marks of sensibility, Sister Frances would have praised the child, but was warned by Madame de Fleury to refrain from injudicious eulogiums, lest she should teach her affectation.

"If I must not praise, you will permit me at least to love her," said Sister Frances.

Her affection for Victoire was increased by compassion: during two months the poor child's arm hung in a sling, so that she could not venture to play with her companions. At their hours of recreation she used to sit on the schoolroom steps, looking down into the garden at the scene of merriment in which she could not partake.

For those who know how to find it, there is good in everything. Sister Frances used to take her seat on the steps, sometimes with her work and sometimes with a book; and Victoire, tired of being quite idle, listened with eagerness to the stories which Sister Frances read, or watched with interest the progress of her work; soon she longed to imitate what she saw done with so much pleasure, and begged to be taught to work and read. By degrees she learned her alphabet, and could soon, to the amazement of her schoolfellows, read the names of all the animals in Sister Frances' picture-book. No matter how trifling the thing done, or the knowledge acquired, a great point is gained by giving the desire for employment. Children frequently become industrious from impatience of the pains and penalties of idleness. Count Rumford showed that he understood childish nature perfectly well when, in his House of Industry at Munich, he compelled the young children to sit for some time idle in a gallery round the hall, where others a little older than themselves were busied at work. During Victoire's state of idle convalescence she acquired the desire to be employed, and she consequently soon became more industrious than her neighbours. Succeeding in her first efforts, she was praised—was pleased, and persevered till she became an example of activity to her companions. But Victoire, though now nearly seven years old, was not quite perfect. Naturally, or accidentally, she was very passionate, and not a little self-willed.

One day being mounted, horsemanlike, with whip in hand, upon the banister of the flight of stairs leading from the schoolroom to the garden, she called in a tone of triumph to her playfellows, desiring them to stand out of the way, and see her slide from top to bottom. At this moment Sister Frances came to the schoolroom door and forbade the feat; but Victoire, regardless of all prohibition, slid down instantly, and moreover was going to repeat the glorious operation, when Sister Frances, catching hold of her arm, pointed to a heap of sharp stones that lay on the ground upon the other side of the banisters.

"I am not afraid," said Victoire.

"But if you fall there, you may break your arm again."

"And if I do, I can bear it," said Victoire. "Let me go, pray let me go: I must do it."

"No; I forbid you, Victoire, to slide down again. Babet and all the little ones would follow your example, and perhaps break their necks."

The nun, as she spoke, attempted to compel Victoire to dismount; but she was so much of a heroine, that she would do nothing upon compulsion. Clinging fast to the banisters, she resisted with all her might; she kicked and screamed, and screamed and kicked, but at last her feet were taken prisoners; then grasping the railway with one hand, with the other she brandished high the little whip.

"What!" said the mild nun, "would you strike me with that arm?"

The arm dropped instantly—Victoire recollected Madame de Fleury's kindness the day when the arm was broken; dismounting immediately, she threw herself upon her knees in the midst of the crowd of young spectators, and begged pardon of Sister Frances. For the rest of the day she was as gentle as a lamb; nay, some assert that the effects of her contrition were visible during the remainder of the week.

Having thus found the secret of reducing the little rebel to obedience by touching her on the tender point of gratitude, the nun had recourse to this expedient in all perilous cases; but one day, when she was boasting of the infallible operation of her charm, Madame de Fleury advised her to forbear recurring to it frequently, lest she should wear out the sensibility she so much loved. In consequence of this counsel, Victoire's violence of temper was sometimes reduced by force and sometimes corrected by reason; but the principle and the feeling of gratitude were not exhausted or weakened in the struggle.

The hope of reward operated upon her generous mind more powerfully than the fear of punishment; and Madame de Fleury devised rewards with as much ability as some legislators invent punishments.

Victoire's brother Maurice, who was now of an age to earn his own bread, had a strong desire to be bound apprentice to the smith who worked in the house where his mother lodged. This most ardent wish of his soul he had imparted to his sister; and she consulted her benefactress, whom she considered as all-powerful in this, as in every other affair.

"Your brother's wish shall be gratified," replied Madame de Fleury, "if you can keep your temper one month. If you are never in a passion for a whole month, I will undertake that your brother shall be bound apprentice to his friend the smith. To your companions, to Sister Frances, and above all to yourself, I trust, to make me a just report this day month."

CHAPTER IV

"You she preferred to all the gay resorts,
Where female vanity might wish to shine,
The pomp of cities, and the pride of courts."
—*LYTTELTON.*

At the end of the time prescribed, the judges, including Victoire herself, who was the most severe of them all, agreed she had justly deserved her reward. Maurice obtained his wish; and Victoire's temper never relapsed into its former bad habits—so powerful is the effect of a well-chosen motive! Perhaps the historian may be blamed for dwelling on such trivial anecdotes; yet a lady, who was accustomed to the conversation of deep philosophers and polished courtiers, listened without disdain to these simple annals. Nothing appeared to her a trifle that could tend to form the habits of temper, truth, honesty, order, and industry: habits which are to be early induced, not by solemn precepts, but by practical lessons. A few more examples of these shall be recorded, notwithstanding the fear of being tiresome.

One day little Babet, who was now five years old, saw, as she was coming to school, an old woman sitting at a corner of the street beside a large black brazier full of roasted chestnuts. Babet thought that the chestnuts looked and smelled very good; the old woman was talking earnestly to some people, who were on her other side; Babet filled her work-bag with chestnuts, and then ran after her mother and sister, who, having turned the corner of the street, had not seen what passed. When Babet came to the schoolroom, she opened her bag with triumph, displayed her treasure, and offered to divide it with her companions. "Here, Victoire," said she, "here is the largest chestnut for you."

But Victoire would not take it; for she staid that Babet had no money, and that she could not have come honestly by these chestnuts. She spoke so forcibly upon this point that even those who had the tempting morsel actually at their lips forbore to bite; those who had bitten laid down their half-eaten prize; and those who had their hands full of chestnuts rolled them back again towards the bag. Babet cried with vexation.

"I burned my fingers in getting them for you, and now you won't eat them!—And I must not eat them!" said she: then curbing her passion, she added, "But at any rate, I won't be a thief. I am sure I did not think it was being a thief just to take a few chestnuts from an old woman who had such heaps and heaps; but Victoire says it is wrong, and I would not be a thief for all the chestnuts in the world—I'll throw them all into the fire this minute!"

"No; give them back again to the old woman," said Victoire.

"But, may be, she would scold me for having taken them," said Babet; "or who knows but she might whip me?"

"And if she did, could you not bear it?" said Victoire. "I am sure I would rather bear twenty whippings than be a thief."

"Twenty, whippings! that's a great many," said Babet; "and I am so little, consider—and that woman has such a monstrous arm!—Now, if it was Sister Frances, it would be another thing. But come! if you will go with me, Victoire, you shall see how I will behave."

"We will all go with you," said Victoire.

"Yes, all!" said the children; "And Sister Frances, I dare say, would go, if you asked her."

Babet ran and told her, and she readily consented to accompany the little penitent to make restitution. The chestnut woman did not whip Babet, nor even scold her, but said she was sure that since the child was so honest as to return what she had taken, she would never steal again. This was the most glorious day of Babet's life, and the happiest. When the circumstance was told to Madame de Fleury, she gave the little girl a bag of the best chestnuts the old women could select, and Babet with great delight shared her reward with her companions.

"But, alas! these chestnuts are not roasted. Oh, if we could but roast them!" said the children.

Sister Frances placed in the middle of the table on which the chestnuts were spread a small earthenware furnace—a delightful toy, commonly used by children in Paris to cook their little feasts.

"This can be bought for sixpence," said she: "and if each of you twelve earn one halfpenny apiece to-day, you can purchase it to-night, and I will put a little fire into it, and you will then be able to roast your chestnuts."

The children ran eagerly to their work—some to wind worsted for a woman who paid them a liard for each ball, others to shell peas for a neighbouring traiteur—all rejoicing that they were able to earn something. The older girls, under the directions and with the assistance of Sister Frances, completed making, washing, and ironing, half a dozen little caps, to supply a baby-linen warehouse. At the end of the day, when the sum of the produce of their labours was added together, they were surprised to find that, instead of one, they could purchase two furnaces. They received and enjoyed the reward of their united industry. The success of their first efforts was fixed in their memory: for they were very happy roasting the chestnuts, and they were all (Sister Frances inclusive) unanimous in opinion that no chestnuts ever were so good, or so well roasted. Sister Frances always partook in their little innocent amusements; and it was her great delight to be the dispenser of rewards which at once conferred present pleasure and cherished future virtue.

CHAPTER V

"To virtue wake the pulses of the heart,
And bid the tear of emulation start."
—ROGERS.

Victoire, who gave constant exercise to the benevolent feelings of the amiable nun, became every day more dear to her. Far from having the selfishness of a favourite, Victoire loved to bring into public notice the good actions of her companions. "Stoop down your ear to me, Sister Frances," said she, "and I will tell you a secret—I will tell you why my friend Annette is growing so thin—I found it out this morning—she does not eat above half her soup every day. Look, there's her porringer covered up in the corner—she carries it home to her mother, who is sick, and who has not bread to eat."

Madame de Fleury came in whilst Sister Frances was yet bending down to hear this secret; it was repeated to her, and she immediately ordered that a certain allowance of bread should be given to Annette every day to carry to her mother during her illness.

"I give it in charge to you, Victoire, to remember this, and I am sure it will never be forgotten. Here is an order for you upon my baker: run and show it to Annette. This is a pleasure you deserve; I am glad that you have chosen for your friend a girl who is so good a daughter. Good daughters make good friends."

By similar instances of goodness Victoire obtained the love and confidence of her companions, notwithstanding her manifest superiority. In their turn, they were eager to proclaim her merits; and, as Sister Frances and Madame de Fleury administered justice with invariable impartiality, the hateful passions of envy and jealousy were never excited in this little society. No servile sycophant, no malicious detractor, could rob or defraud their little virtues of their due reward.

"Whom shall I trust to take this to Madame de Fleury?" said Sister Frances, carrying into the garden where the children were playing a pot of fine jonquils, which she had brought from her convent.— "These are the first jonquils I have seen this year, and finer I never beheld! Whom shall I trust to take them to Madame de Fleury this evening?—It must be some one who will not stop to stare about on the way, but who will be very, very careful—some one in whom I can place perfect dependence."

"It must be Victoire, then," cried every voice.

"Yes, she deserves it to-day particularly," said Annette eagerly; "because she was not angry with Babet when she did what was enough to put anybody in a passion. Sister Frances, you know this cherry-tree which you grafted for Victoire last year, and that was yesterday so full of blossoms—now you see, there is not a blossom left!—Babet plucked them all this morning to make a nosegay."

"But she did not know," said Victoire, "that pulling off the blossoms would prevent my having any cherries."

"Oh, I am very sorry I was so foolish," said Babet; "Victoire did not even say a cross word to me."

"Though she was excessively anxious about the cherries," pursued Annette, "because she intended to have given the first she had to Madame de Fleury."

"Victoire, take the jonquils—it is but just," said Sister Frances. "How I do love to hear them all praise her!—I knew what she would be from the first."

With a joyful heart Victoire took the jonquils, promised to carry them with the utmost care, and not to stop to stare on the way. She set out to Madame de Fleury's hotel, which was in La Place de Louis Quinze. It was late in the evening, the lamps were lighting, and as Victoire crossed the Pont de Louis Seize, she stopped to look at the reflection of the lamps in the water, which appeared in succession, as they were lighted, spreading as if by magic along the river. While Victoire leaned over the battlements of the bridge, watching the rising of these stars of fire, a sudden push from the elbow of some rude passenger precipitated her pot of jonquils into the Seine. The sound it made in the water was thunder to the ear of Victoire; she stood for an instant vainly hoping it would rise again, but the waters had closed over it for ever.

"Dans cet etat affreux, que faire?   . . . Mon devoir."

Victoire courageously proceeded to Madame de Fleury's, and desired to see her.

"D'abord c'est impossible—madame is dressing to go to a concert," said Francois. "Cannot you leave your message?"

"Oh no," said Victoire; "it is of great consequence—I must see her myself; and she is so good, and you too, Monsieur Francois, that I am sure you will not refuse."

"Well, I remember one day you found the seal of my watch, which I dropped at your schoolroom door—one good turn deserves another. If it is possible it shall be done—I will inquire of madame's woman."—"Follow me upstairs," said he, returning in a few minutes; "madame will see you."

She followed him up the large staircase, and through a suite of apartments sufficiently grand to intimidate her young imagination.

"Madame est dans son cabinet. Entrez—mais entrez donc, entrez toujours."

Madame de Fleury was more richly dressed than usual; and her image was reflected in the large looking-glass, so that at the first moment Victoire thought she saw many fine ladies, but not one of them the lady she wanted.

"Well, Victoire, my child, what is the matter?"

"Oh, it is her voice!—I know you now, madame, and I am not afraid—not afraid even to tell you how foolish I have been. Sister Frances trusted me to carry for you, madame, a beautiful pot of jonquils, and she desired me not to stop on the way to stare; but I did stop to look at the lamps on the bridge, and I forgot the jonquils, and somebody brushed by me and threw them into the river—and I am very sorry I was so foolish."

"And I am very glad that you are so wise as to tell the truth, without attempting to make any paltry excuses. Go home to Sister Frances, and assure her that I am more obliged to her for making you such an honest girl than I could be for a whole bed of jonquils."

Victoire's heart was so full that she could not speak—she kissed Madame de Fleury's hand in silence, and then seemed to be lost in contemplation of her bracelet.

"Are you thinking, Victoire, that you should be much happier if you had such bracelets as these? Believe me, you are mistaken if you think so; many people are unhappy who wear fine bracelets; so, my child, content yourself."

"Myself! Oh, madame, I was not thinking of myself—I was not wishing for bracelets; I was only thinking that—"

"That what?"

"That it is a pity you are so very rich; you have everything in this world that you want, and I can never be of the least use to you—all my life I shall never be able to do you any good—and what," said Victoire, turning away to hide her tears, "what signifies the gratitude of such a poor little creature as I am?"

"Did you never hear the fable of the lion and the mouse, Victoire?"

"No, madame—never!"

"Then I will tell it to you."

Victoire looked up with eyes of eager expectation—Francois opened the door to announce that the Marquis de M— and the Comte de S— were in the saloon; but Madame de Fleury stayed to tell Victoire her fable—she would not lose the opportunity of making an impression upon this child's heart.

It is whilst the mind is warm that the deepest impressions can be made. Seizing the happy moment sometimes decides the character and the fate of a child. In this respect, what advantages have the rich and great in educating the children of the poor! they have the power which their rank and all its decorations obtain over the imagination. Their smiles are favours; their words are listened to as oracular; they are looked up to as beings of a superior order. Their powers of working good are almost as great, though not quite so wonderful, as those formerly attributed to beneficent, fairies.

CHAPTER VI

"Knowledge for them unlocks her useful page,
And virtue blossoms for a better age."
—BARBAULD.

A few days after Madame de Fleury had told Victoire the fable of the lion and the mouse, she was informed by Sister Frances that Victoire had put the fable into verse. It was wonderfully well done for a child of nine years old, and Madame de Fleury was tempted to praise the lines; but, checking the enthusiasm of the moment, she considered whether it would be advantageous to cultivate her pupil's talent for poetry. Excellence in the poetic art cannot be obtained without a degree of application for which a girl in her situation could not have leisure. To encourage her to become a mere rhyming scribbler, without any chance of obtaining celebrity or securing subsistence, would be folly and cruelty. Early prodigies in the lower ranks of life are seldom permanently successful; they are cried up one day, and cried down the next. Their productions rarely have that superiority which secures a fair preference in the great literary market. Their performances are, perhaps, said to be wonderful, all things considered, &c. Charitable allowances are made; the books are purchased by associations of complaisant friends or opulent patrons; a kind of forced demand is raised, but this can be only temporary and delusive. In spite of bounties and of all the arts of protection, nothing but what is intrinsically good will long be preferred, when it must be purchased. But granting that positive excellence is attained, there is always danger that for works of fancy the taste of the public may suddenly vary: there is a fashion in these things; and when the mode changes, the mere literary manufacturer is thrown out of employment; he is unable to turn his hand to another trade, or to any but his own peculiar branch of the business. The powers of the mind are often partially cultivated in these self-taught geniuses. We often see that one part of their understanding is nourished to the prejudice of the rest—the imagination, for instance, at the expense of the judgment: so that whilst they have acquired talents for show they have none for use. In the affairs of common life they are utterly ignorant and imbecile—or worse than imbecile. Early called into public notice, probably before their moral habits are formed, they are extolled for some play of fancy or of wit, as Bacon calls it, some juggler's trick of the intellect; they immediately take an aversion to plodding labour, they feel raised above their situation; possessed by the notion that genius exempts them not only from labour, but from vulgar rules of prudence, they soon disgrace themselves by their conduct, are deserted by their patrons, and sink into despair or plunge into profligacy.

Convinced of these melancholy truths, Madame de Fleury was determined not to add to the number of those imprudent or ostentatious patrons, who sacrifice to their own amusement and vanity the future happiness of their favourites. Victoire's verses were not handed about in fashionable circles, nor was she called upon to recite them before a brilliant audience, nor was she produced in public as a prodigy; she was educated in private, and by slow and sure degrees, to be a good, useful, and happy member of society. Upon the same principles which decided Madame de Fleury against encouraging Victoire to be a poetess, she refrained from giving any of her little pupils accomplishments unsuited to their situation. Some had a fine ear for music, others showed powers of dancing; but they were taught neither dancing nor music—talents which in their station were more likely to be dangerous than serviceable. They were not intended for actresses or opera-girls, but for shop-girls, mantua-makers, work-women, and servants of different sorts; consequently they were instructed in things which would be most necessary and useful to young women in their rank of life. Before they were ten years old they could do all kinds of plain needlework, they could read and write well, and they were mistresses of the common rules of arithmetic. After this age they were practised by a writing-master in drawing out bills neatly, keeping accounts, and applying to every-day use their knowledge of arithmetic. Some were taught by a laundress to wash and get up fine linen and lace; others were instructed by a neighbouring traiteur in those culinary mysteries with which Sister Frances was unacquainted. In sweetmeats and confectioneries she yielded to no one; and she made her pupils as expert as herself. Those who were intended for ladies' maids were taught mantua-making, and had lessons from Madame de Fleury's own woman in hairdressing.

Amongst her numerous friends and acquaintances, and amongst the shopkeepers whom she was in the habit of employing, Madame de Fleury had means of placing and establishing her pupils suitably and advantageously: of this, both they and their parents were aware, so that there was a constant and great motive operating continually to induce them to exert themselves, and to behave well. This reasonable hope of reaping the fruits of their education, and of being immediately rewarded for their good conduct;

this perception of the connection between what they are taught and what they are to become, is necessary to make young people assiduous; for want of attending to these principles many splendid establishments have failed to produce pupils answerable to the expectations which had been formed of them.

During seven years that Madame de Fleury persevered uniformly on the same plan, only one girl forfeited her protection—a girl of the name of Manon; she was Victoire's cousin, but totally unlike her in character.

When very young, her beautiful eyes and hair caught the fancy of a rich lady, who took her into her family as a sort of humble playfellow for her children. She was taught to dance and to sing: she soon excelled in these accomplishments, and was admired, and produced as a prodigy of talent. The lady of the house gave herself great credit for having discerned, and having brought forward, such talents. Manon's moral character was in the meantime neglected. In this house, where there was a constant scene of hurry and dissipation, the child had frequent opportunities and temptations to be dishonest. For some time she was not detected; her caressing manners pleased her patroness, and servile compliance with the humours of the children of the family secured their goodwill. Encouraged by daily petty successes in the art of deceit, she became a complete hypocrite. With culpable negligence, her mistress trusted implicitly to appearances; and without examining whether she were really honest, she suffered her to have free access to unlocked drawers and valuable cabinets. Several articles of dress were missed from time to time; but Manon managed so artfully, that she averted from herself all suspicion. Emboldened by this fatal impunity, she at last attempted depredations of more importance. She purloined a valuable snuff-box—was detected in disposing of the broken parts of it at a pawnbroker's, and was immediately discarded in disgrace; but by her tears and vehement expressions of remorse she so far worked upon the weakness of the lady of the house as to prevail upon her to conceal the circumstance that occasioned her dismissal. Some months afterwards, Manon, pleading that she was thoroughly reformed, obtained from this lady a recommendation to Madame de Fleury's school. It is wonderful that, people, who in other respects profess and practise integrity, can be so culpably weak as to give good characters to those who do not deserve them: this is really one of the worst species of forgery. Imposed upon by this treacherous recommendation, Madame de Fleury received into the midst of her innocent young pupils one who might have corrupted their minds secretly and irrecoverably. Fortunately a discovery was made in time of Manon's real disposition. A mere trifle led to the detection of her habits of falsehood. As she could not do any kind of needlework, she was employed in winding cotton; she was negligent, and did not in the course of the week wind the same number of balls as her companions; and to conceal this, she pretended that she had delivered the proper number to the woman, who regularly called at the end of the week for the cotton. The woman persisted in her account, and the children in theirs; and Manon would not retract her assertion. The poor woman gave up the point; but she declared that she would the next time send her brother to make up the account, because he was sharper than herself, and would not be imposed upon so easily. The ensuing week the brother came, and he proved to be the very pawnbroker to whom Manon formerly offered the stolen box: he knew her immediately; it was in vain that she attempted to puzzle him, and to persuade him that she was not the same person. The man was clear and firm. Sister Frances could scarcely believe what she heard. Struck with horror, the children shrank back from Manon, and stood in silence. Madame de Fleury immediately wrote to the lady who had recommended this girl, and inquired into the truth of the pawnbroker's assertions. The lady, who had given Manon a false character, could not deny the facts, and could apologise for herself only by saying that "she believed the girl to be partly reformed, and that she hoped, under Madame de Fleury's judicious care, she would become an amiable and respectable woman."

Madame de Fleury, however, wisely judged that the hazard of corrupting all her pupils should not be incurred for the slight chance of correcting one, whose bad habits wore of such long standing. Manon was expelled from this happy little community—even Sister Frances, the most mild of human beings, could never think of the danger to which they had been exposed without expressing indignation against the lady who recommended such a girl as a fit companion for her blameless and beloved pupils.

CHAPTER VII

"Alas! regardless of their doom,
The little victims play:
No sense have they of ills to come,
No care beyond to-day."
—GRAY.

Good legislators always attend to the habits, and what is called the genius, of the people they have to govern. From youth to age, the taste for whatever is called une fete pervades the whole French nation. Madame de Fleury availed herself judiciously of this powerful motive, and connected it with the feelings of affection more than with the passion for show. For instance, when any of her little people had done anything particularly worthy of reward, she gave them leave to invite their parents to a fete prepared for them by their children, assisted by the kindness of Sister Frances.

One day—it was a holiday obtained by Victoire's good conduct—all the children prepared in their garden a little feast for their parents. Sister Frances spread the table with a bountiful hand, the happy fathers and mothers were waited upon by their children, and each in their turn heard with delight from the benevolent nun some instance of their daughter's improvement. Full of hope for the future and of gratitude for the past, these honest people ate and talked, whilst in imagination they saw their children all prosperously and usefully settled in the world. They blessed Madame de Fleury in her absence, and they wished ardently for her presence.

"The sun is setting, and Madame de Fleury is not yet come," cried Victoire; "she said she would be here this evening—What can be the matter?"

"Nothing is the matter, you may be sure," said Babet; "but that she has forgotten us—she has so many things to think of."

"Yes; but I know she never forgets us," said Victoire; "and she loves so much to see us all happy together, that I am sure it must be something very extraordinary that detains her."

Babet laughed at Victoire's fears; but presently even she began to grow impatient; for they waited long after sunset, expecting every moment that Madame de Fleury would arrive. At last she appeared, but with a dejected countenance, which seemed to justify Victoire's foreboding. When she saw this festive company, each child sitting between her parents, and all at her entrance looking up with affectionate pleasure, a faint smile enlivened her countenance for a moment; but she did not speak to them with her usual ease. Her mind seemed preoccupied by some disagreeable business of importance. It appeared that it had some connection with them; for as she walked round the table with Sister Frances, she said, with a voice and look of great tenderness, "Poor children! how happy they are at this moment!—Heaven only knows how soon they may be rendered, or may render themselves, miserable!"

None of the children could imagine what this meant; but their parents guessed that it had some allusion to the state of public affairs. About this time some of those discontents had broken out which preceded the terrible days of the Revolution. As yet, most of the common people, who were honestly employed in earning their own living, neither understood what was going on nor foresaw what was to happen. Many of their superiors were not in such happy ignorance—they had information of the intrigues that were forming; and the more penetration they possessed, the more they feared the consequences of events which they could not control. At the house of a great man, with whom she had dined this day, Madame de Fleury had heard alarming news. Dreadful public disturbances, she saw, were inevitable; and whilst she trembled for the fate of all who were dear to her, these poor children had a share in her anxiety. She foresaw the temptations, the dangers, to which they must be exposed, whether they abandoned, or whether they abided by the principles their education had instilled. She feared that the labour of years would perhaps be lost in an instant, or that her innocent pupils would fall victims even to their virtues.

Many of these young people were now of an age to understand and to govern themselves by reason; and with these she determined to use those preventive measures which reason affords. Without meddling with politics, in which no amiable or sensible woman can wish to interfere, the influence of ladies in the higher ranks of life may always be exerted with perfect propriety, and with essential advantage to the public, in conciliating the inferior classes of society, explaining to them their duties and their interests, and impressing upon the minds of the children of the poor sentiments of just subordination and honest independence. How happy would it have been for France if women of fortune and abilities had always exerted their talents and activity in this manner, instead of wasting their powers in futile declamations, or in the intrigues of party!

CHAPTER VIII

"E'en now the devastation is begun,
And half the business of destruction done."
—GOLDSMITH.

Madame de Fleury was not disappointed in her pupils. When the public disturbances began, these children were shocked by the horrible actions they saw. Instead of being seduced by bad example, they only showed anxiety to avoid companions of their own age who were dishonest, idle, or profligate. Victoire's cousin Manon ridiculed these absurd principles, as she called them, and endeavoured to persuade Victoire that she would be much happier if she followed the fashion.

"What! Victoire, still with your work-bag on your arm, and still going to school with your little sister, though you are but a year younger than I am, I believe!—thirteen last birthday, were not you?—Mon Dieu! Why, how long do you intend to be a child? and why don't you leave that old nun, who keeps you in leading-strings?—I assure you, nuns, and school- mistresses, and schools, and all that sort of thing, are out of fashion now—we have abolished all that—we are to live a life of reason now—and all soon to be equal, I can tell you; let your Madame de Fleury look to that, and look to it yourself; for with all your wisdom, you might find yourself in the wrong box by sticking to her, and that side of the question.—

Disengage yourself from her, I advise you, as soon as you can.—My dear Victoire! believe me, you may spell very well—but you know nothing of the rights of man, or the rights of woman."

"I do not pretend to know anything of the rights of men, or the rights of women," cried Victoire; "but this I know: that I never can or will be ungrateful to Madame de Fleury. Disengage myself from her! I am bound to her for ever, and I will abide by her till the last hour I breathe."

"Well, well! there is no occasion to be in a passion—I only speak as a friend, and I have no more time to reason with you; for I must go home, and get ready my dress for the ball to-night."

"Manon, how can you afford to buy a dress for a ball?"

"As you might, if you had common sense, Victoire—only by being a good citizen. I and a party of us denounced a milliner and a confectioner in our neighbourhood, who were horrible aristocrats; and of their goods forfeited to the nation we had, as was our just share, such delicious marangues and charming ribands!—Oh, Victoire, believe me, you will never get such things by going to school, or saying your prayers either. You may look with as much scorn and indignation as you please, but I advise you to let it alone, for all that is out of fashion, and may, moreover, bring you into difficulties. Believe me, my dear Victoire, your head is not deep enough to understand these things—you know nothing of politics."

"But I know the difference between right and wrong, Manon: politics can never alter that, you know."

"Never alter that! there you are quite mistaken," said Manon. "I cannot stay to convince you now—but this I can tell you: that I know secrets that you don't suspect."

"I do not wish to know any of your secrets, Manon," said Victoire, proudly.

"Your pride may be humbled, Citoyenne Victoire, sooner than you expect," exclaimed Manon, who was now so provoked by her cousin's contempt that she could not refrain from boasting of her political knowledge. "I can tell you that your fine friends will in a few days not be able to protect you. The Abbe Tracassier is in love with a dear friend of mine, and I know all the secrets of state from her—and I know what I know. Be as incredulous as you please, but you will see that, before this week is at end, Monsieur de Fleury will be guillotined, and then what will become of you? Good morning, my proud cousin."

Shocked by what she had just heard, Victoire could scarcely believe that Manon was in earnest; she resolved, however, to go immediately and communicate this intelligence, whether true or false, to Madame de Fleury. It agreed but too well with other circumstances, which alarmed this lady for the safety of her husband. A man of his abilities, integrity, and fortune, could not in such times hope to escape persecution. He was inclined to brave the danger; but his lady represented that it would not be courage, but rashness and folly, to sacrifice his life to the villainy of others, without probability or possibility of serving his country by his fall.

Monsieur de Fleury, in consequence of these representations, and of Victoire's intelligence, made his escape from Paris; and the very next day placards were put up in every street, offering a price for the head of Citoyen Fleury, suspected of incivisme.

Struck with terror and astonishment at the sight of these placards, the children read them as they returned in the evening from school; and little Babet in the vehemence of her indignation mounted a lamplighter's ladder, and tore down one of the papers. This imprudent action did not pass unobserved: it was seen by one of the spies of Citoyen Tracassier, a man who, under the pretence of zeal pour la chose publique, gratified without scruple his private resentments and his malevolent passions. In his former character of an abbe, and a man of wit, he had gained admittance into Madame de Fleury's society. There he attempted to dictate both as a literary and religious despot. Accidentally discovering that Madame de Fleury had a little school for poor children, he thought proper to be offended, because he had not been consulted respecting the regulations, and because he was not permitted, as he said, to take the charge of this little flock. He made many objections to Sister Frances, as being an improper person to have the spiritual guidance of these young people; but as he was unable to give any just reason for his dislike, Madame de Fleury persisted in her choice, and was at last obliged to assert, in opposition to the domineering abbe, her right to judge and decide in her own affairs. With seeming politeness, he begged ten thousand pardons for his conscientious interference. No more was said upon the subject; and as he did not totally withdraw from her society till the revolution broke out, she did not suspect that she had anything to fear from his resentment. His manners and opinions changed suddenly with the times; the mask of religion was thrown off; and now, instead of objecting to Sister Frances as not being sufficiently strict and orthodox in her tenets, he boldly declared that a nun was not a fit person to be intrusted with the education of any of the young citizens—they should all be des eleves de la patrie. The abbe, become a member of the Committee of Public Safety, denounced Madame de Fleury, in the strange jargon of the day, as "the fosterer of a swarm of bad citizens, who were nourished in the anticivic prejudices de l'ancien regime, and fostered in the most detestable superstitions, in defiance of the law." He further observed, that he had good reason to believe that some of these little enemies to the constitution had contrived and abetted Monsieur de Fleury's escape. Of their having rejoiced at it in a most indecent manner, he said he could produce irrefragable proof. The boy who saw Babet tear down the placard was produced and solemnly examined; and the thoughtless action of this poor little girl was construed into a state crime of the most horrible nature. In a declamatory tone, Tracassier reminded his fellow-citizens, that in the ancient Grecian times of virtuous republicanism (times of which France ought to show herself emulous), an Athenian child was condemned to death for having made a plaything of a fragment of the gilding that had fallen from a public statue. The orator, for the reward of his eloquence, obtained an order to seize everything in Madame de Fleury's school-house, and to throw the nun into prison.

CHAPTER IX

"Who now will guard bewildered youth
Safe from the fierce assault of hostile rage?—
Such war can Virtue wage?"

At the very moment when this order was going to be put in execution, Madame de Fleury was sitting in the midst of the children, listening to Babet, who was reading AEsop's fable of The old man and his sons. Whilst her sister was reading, Victoire collected a number of twigs from the garden: she had just tied them together; and was going, by Sister Frances' desire, to let her companions try if they could break the bundle, when the attention to the moral of the fable was interrupted by the entrance of an old woman, whose countenance expressed the utmost terror and haste, to tell what she had not breath to utter. To Madame de Fleury she was a stranger; but the children immediately recollected her to be the chestnut woman to whom Babet had some years ago restored certain purloined chestnuts.

"Fly!" said she, the moment she had breath to speak: "Fly!—they are coming to seize everything here—carry off what you can—make haste—make haste!—I came through a by-street. A man was eating chestnuts at my stall, and I saw him show one that was with him the order from Citoyen Tracassier. They'll be here in five minutes—quick!—quick!—You, in particular," continued she, turning to the nun, "else you'll be in prison."

At these words, the children, who had clung round Sister Frances, loosed their hold, exclaiming, "Go! go quick: but where? where?—we will go with her."

"No, no!" said Madame de Fleury, "she shall come home with me—my carriage is at the door."

"Ma belle dame!" cried the chestnut woman, "your house is the worst place she can go to—let her come to my cellar—the poorest cellar in these days is safer than the grandest palace."

So saying, she seized the nun with honest roughness, and hurried her away. As soon as she was gone, the children ran different ways, each to collect some favourite thing, which they thought they could not leave behind. Victoire alone stood motionless beside Madame de Fleury; her whole thoughts absorbed by the fear that her benefactress would be imprisoned. "Oh, madame! dear, dear Madame de Fleury, don't stay! don't stay!"

"Oh, children, never mind these things."

"Don't stay, madame, don't stay! I will stay with them—I will stay—do you go."

The children hearing these words, and recollecting Madame de Fleury's danger, abandoned all their little property, and instantly obeyed her orders to go home to their parents. Victoire at last saw Madame de Fleury safe in her carriage. The coachman drove off at a great rate; and a few minutes afterwards Tracassier's myrmidons arrived at the school- house. Great was their surprise when they found only the poor children's little books, unfinished samplers, and half-hemmed handkerchiefs. They ran into the garden to search for the nun. They were men of brutal habits, yet as they looked at everything round them, which bespoke peace, innocence, and childish happiness, they could not help thinking it was a pity to destroy what could do the nation no great harm after all. They were even glad that the nun had made her escape, since they were not answerable for it; and they returned to their employer satisfied for once without doing any mischief; but Citizen Tracassier was of too vindictive a temper to suffer the objects of his hatred thus to elude his vengeance. The next day Madame de Fleury was summoned before his tribunal and ordered to give up the nun, against whom, as a suspected person, a decree of the law had been obtained.

Madame de Fleury refused to betray the innocent woman; the gentle firmness of this lady's answers to a brutal interrogatory was termed insolence—she was pronounced a refractory aristocrat, dangerous to the state; and an order was made out to seal up her goods, and to keep her a prisoner in her own house.

CHAPTER X

"Alas! full oft on Guilt's victorious car
The spoils of Virtue are in triumph borne,

A close prisoner in her own house, Madame de Fleury was now guarded by men suddenly become soldiers, and sprung from the dregs of the people; men of brutal manners, ferocious countenances, and more ferocious minds. They seemed to delight in the insolent display of their newly-acquired power. One of those men had formerly been convicted of some horrible crime, and had been sent to the galleys by M. de Fleury. Revenge actuated this wretch under the mask of patriotism, and he rejoiced in seeing the wife of the man he hated a prisoner in his custody. Ignorant of the facts, his associates were ready to believe him in the right, and to join in the senseless cry against all who were their superiors in fortune, birth, and education. This unfortunate lady was forbidden all intercourse with her friends, and it was in vain she attempted to obtain from her gaolers intelligence of what was passing in Paris.

"Tu verras—Tout va bien—Ca ira," were the only answers they deigned to make; frequently they continued smoking their pipes in obdurate silence. She occupied the back rooms of her house, because her guards apprehended that she might from the front windows receive intelligence from her friends. One morning she was awakened by an unusual noise in the streets; and, upon her inquiring the occasion of it, her guards told her she was welcome to go to the front windows and satisfy her curiosity. She went, and saw an immense crowd of people surrounding a guillotine that had been erected the preceding night. Madame de Fleury started back with horror—her guards burst into an inhuman laugh, and asked whether her curiosity was satisfied. She would have left the room; but it was now their pleasure to detain her, and to force her to continue the whole day in this apartment. When the guillotine began its work, they had even the barbarity to drag her to the window, repeating, "It is there you ought to be!—It is there your husband ought to be!—You are too happy, that your husband is not there this moment. But he will be there—the law will overtake him—he will be there in time—and you too!"

The mild fortitude of this innocent, benevolent woman made no impression upon these cruel men. When at night they saw her kneeling at her prayers, they taunted her with gross and impious mockery; and when she sank to sleep, they would waken her by their loud and drunken orgies—if she remonstrated, they answered, "The enemies of the constitution should have no rest."

Madame de Fleury was not an enemy to any human being; she had never interfered in politics; her life had been passed in domestic pleasures, or employed for the good of her fellow-creatures. Even in this hour of personal danger she thought of others more than of herself: she thought of her husband, an exile in a foreign country, who might be reduced to the utmost distress now that she was deprived of all means of remitting him money. She thought of her friends, who, she knew, would exert themselves to obtain her liberty, and whose zeal in her cause might involve them and their families in distress. She thought of the good Sister Frances, who had been exposed by her means to the unrelenting persecution of the malignant and powerful Tracassier. She thought of her poor little pupils, now thrown upon the world without a protector. Whilst these ideas were revolving in her mind one night as she lay awake, she heard the door of her chamber open softly, and a soldier, one of her guards, with a light in his hand, entered; he came to the foot of her bed, and, as she started up, laid his finger upon his lips.

"Don't make the least noise," said he in a whisper; "those without are drunk, and asleep. Don't you know me?—don't you remember my face?"

"Not in the least; yet I have some recollection of your voice."

The man took off the bonnet-rouge—still she could not guess who he was. "You never saw me in a uniform before nor without a black face."

She looked again, and recollected the smith to whom Maurice was bound apprentice, and remembered his patois accent.

"I remember you," said he, "at any rate; and your goodness to that poor girl the day her arm was broken, and all your goodness to Maurice. But I've no time for talking of that now—get up, wrap this great coat round you—don't be in a hurry, but make no noise—and follow me."

She followed him; and he led her past the sleeping sentinels, opened a back door into the garden, hurried her (almost carried her) across the garden to a door at the furthest end of it, which opened into Les Champs Elysees—"La voila!" cried he, pushing her through the half-opened door. "God be praised!" answered a voice, which Madame de Fleury knew to be Victoire's, whose arms were thrown round her with a transport of joy.

"Softly; she is not safe yet—wait till we get her home, Victoire," said another voice, which she knew to be that of Maurice. He produced a dark lantern, and guided Madame de Fleury across the Champs Elysees, and across the bridge, and then through various by-streets, in perfect silence, till they arrived safely at the house where Victoire's mother lodged, and went up those very stairs which she had ascended in such different circumstances several years before. The mother, who was sitting up waiting most anxiously for the return of her children, clasped her hands in an ecstasy when she saw them return with Madame de Fleury.

"Welcome, madame! Welcome, dear madame! but who would have thought of seeing you here in such a way? Let her rest herself—let her rest; she is quite overcome. Here, madame, can you sleep on this poor bed?"

"The very same bed you laid me upon the day my arm was broken," said Victoire.

"Ay, Lord bless her!" said the mother; "and though it's seven good years ago, it seemed but yesterday that I saw her sitting on that bed beside my poor child looking like an angel. But let her rest, let her rest—we'll not say a word more, only God bless her; thank Heaven, she's safe with us at last!"

Madame de Fleury expressed unwillingness to stay with these good people, lest she should expose them to danger; but they begged most earnestly that she would remain with them without scruple.

"Surely, madame," said the mother, "you must think that we have some remembrance of all you have done for us, and some touch of gratitude."

"And surely, madame, you can trust us, I hope," said Maurice.

"And surely you are not too proud to let us do something for you. The lion was not too proud to be served by the poor little mouse," said Victoire. "As to danger for us," continued she, "there can be none; for Maurice and I have contrived a hiding-place for you, madame, that can never be found out—

let them come spying here as often as they please, they will never find her out, will they, Maurice? Look, madame, into this lumber-room; you see it seems to be quite full of wood for firing; well, if you creep in behind, you can hide yourself quite sung in the loft above, and here's a trap-door into the loft that nobody ever would think of, for we have hung these old things from the top of it, and who could guess it was a trap-door? So you see, dear madame, you may sleep in peace here, and never fear for us."

Though but a girl of fourteen, Victoire showed at this time all the sense and prudence of a woman of thirty. Gratitude seemed at once to develop all the powers of her mind. It was she and Maurice who had prevailed upon the smith to effect Madame de Fleury's escape from her own house. She had invented, she had foreseen, she had arranged everything; she had scarcely rested night or day since the imprisonment of her benefactress, and now that her exertions had fully succeeded, her joy seemed to raise her above all feeling of fatigue; she looked as fresh and moved as briskly, her mother said, as if she were preparing to go to a ball.

"Ah! my child," said she, "your cousin Manon, who goes to those balls every night, was never so happy as you are this minute."

But Victoire's happiness was not of long continuance; for the next day they were alarmed by intelligence that Tracassier was enraged beyond measure at Madame de Fleury's escape, that all his emissaries were at work to discover her present hiding-place, that the houses of all the parents and relations of her pupils were to be searched, and that the most severe denunciations were issued against all by whom she should be harboured. Manon was the person who gave this intelligence, but not with any benevolent design; she first came to Victoire, to display her own consequence; and to terrify her, she related all she knew from a soldier's wife, who was M. Tracassier's mistress. Victoire had sufficient command over herself to conceal from the inquisitive eyes of Manon the agitation of her heart; she had also the prudence not to let any one of her companions into her secret, though, when she saw their anxiety, she was much tempted to relieve them, by the assurance that Madame de Fleury was in safety. All the day was passed in apprehension. Madame de Fleury never stirred from her place of concealment: as the evening and the hour of the domiciliary visits approached, Victoire and Maurice were alarmed by an unforeseen difficulty. Their mother, whose health had been broken by hard work, in vain endeavoured to suppress her terror at the thoughts of this domiciliary visit; she repeated incessantly that she knew they should all be discovered, and that her children would be dragged to the guillotine before her face. She was in such a distracted state, that they dreaded she would, the moment she saw the soldiers, reveal all she knew.

"If they question me, I shall not know what to answer," cried the terrified woman. "What can I say?— What can I do?"

Reasoning, entreaties, all were vain; she was not in a condition to understand, or even to listen to, anything that was said. In this situation they were when the domiciliary visitors arrived—they heard the noise of the soldiers' feet on the stairs—the poor woman sprang from the arms of her children; but at the moment the door was opened, and she saw the glittering of the bayonets, she fell at full length in a swoon on the floor—fortunately before she had power to utter a syllable. The people of the house knew, and said, that she was subject to fits on any sudden alarm; so that her being affected in this manner did not appear surprising. They threw her on a bed, whilst they proceeded to search the house: her children stayed with her; and, wholly occupied in attending to her, they were not exposed to the danger of betraying their anxiety about Madame de Fleury. They trembled, however, from head to foot when they heard one of the soldiers swear that all the wood in the lumber-room must be pulled out, and that he would not leave the house till every stick was moved; the sound of each log, as it was thrown out, was heard by Victoire; her brother was now summoned to assist. How great was his terror when one of the searchers looked up to the roof, as if expecting to find a trap door; fortunately, however, he did not discover it. Maurice, who had seized the light, contrived to throw the shadows so as to deceive the eye. The soldiers at length retreated; and with inexpressible satisfaction Maurice lighted them down stairs, and saw them fairly out of the house. For some minutes after they were in safety, the terrified mother, who had recovered her senses, could scarcely believe that the danger was over. She embraced her children by turns with wild transport; and with tears begged Madame de Fleury to forgive her cowardice, and not to attribute it to ingratitude, or to suspect that she had a bad heart. She protested that she was now become so courageous, since she found that she had gone through this trial successfully, and since she was sure that the hiding-place was really so secure, that she should never be alarmed at any domiciliary visit in future. Madame de Fleury, however, did not think it either just or expedient to put her resolution to the trial. She determined to leave Paris; and, if possible, to make her escape from France. The master of one of the Paris diligences was brother to Francois, her footman: he was ready to assist her at all hazards, and to convey her safely to Bourdeaux, if she could disguise herself properly; and if she could obtain a pass from any friend under a feigned name.

Victoire—the indefatigable Victoire—recollected that her friend Annette had an aunt, who was nearly of Madame de Fleury's size, and who had just obtained a pass to go to Bourdeaux, to visit some of her relations. The pass was willingly given up to Madame de Fleury; and upon reading it over it was found to answer tolerably well—the colour of the eyes and hair at least would do; though the words un nez gros were not precisely descriptive of this lady's. Annette's mother, who had always worn the provincial dress of Auvergne, furnished the high cornette, stiff stays, bodice, &c.; and equipped in these, Madame de Fleury was so admirably well disguised, that even Victoire declared she should scarcely have known her. Money, that most necessary passport in all countries, was still wanting: as seals had been put upon all Madame de Fleury's effects the day she had been first imprisoned in her own house, she could not save even her jewels. She had, however, one ring on her finger of some value. How to dispose of it without exciting suspicion was the difficulty. Babet, who was resolved to have her share in assisting her benefactress, proposed to carry the ring to a colporteur—a pedlar, or sort of travelling jeweller—who had come to lay in a stock of hardware at Paris: he was related to one of Madame de Fleury's little pupils, and readily disposed of the ring for her: she obtained at least two-thirds of its value—a great deal in those times.

The proofs of integrity, attachment, and gratitude which she received in these days of peril, from those whom she had obliged in her prosperity, touched her generous heart so much, that she has often since declared she could not regret having been reduced to distress. Before she quitted Paris she wrote letters to her friends, recommending her pupils to their protection; she left these letters in the care of Victoire, who to the last moment followed her with anxious affection. She would have followed her benefactress into exile, but that she was prevented by duty and affection from leaving her mother, who was in declining health.

Madame de Fleury successfully made her escape from Paris. Some of the municipal officers in the towns through which she passed on her road were as severe as their ignorance would permit in scrutinising her passport. It seldom happened that more than one of these petty committees of public safety could read. One usually spelled out the passport as well as he could, whilst the others smoked their pipes, and from time to time held a light up to the lady's face to examine whether it agreed with the description.

"Mais toi! tu n'as pas le nez gros!" said one of her judges to her. "Son nez est assez gros, et c'est moi qui le dit," said another. The question was put to the vote; and the man who had asserted what was contrary to the evidence of his senses was so vehement in supporting his opinion, that it was carried in spite of all that could be said against it. Madame de Fleury was suffered to proceed on her journey. She reached Bordeaux in safety. Her husband's friends—the good have always friends in adversity—her husband's friends exerted themselves for her with the most prudent zeal. She was soon provided with a sum of money sufficient for her support for some time in England; and she safely reached that free and happy country, which has been the refuge of so many illustrious exiles.

CHAPTER XI

"Cosi rozzo diamante appena splende
Dalla rupe natia quand' esce fuora,
E a poco a poco lucido se rende
Sotto l'attenta che lo lavora."

Madame de Fleury joined her husband, who was in London, and they both lived in the most retired and frugal manner. They had too much of the pride of independence to become burthensome to their generous English friends. Notwithstanding the variety of difficulties they had to encounter, and the number of daily privations to which they were forced to submit, yet they were happy—in a tranquil conscience, in their mutual affection, and the attachment of many poor but grateful friends. A few months after she came to England, Madame de Fleury received, by a private hand, a packet of letters from her little pupils. Each of them, even the youngest, who had but just begun to learn joining-hand, would write a few lines in this packet.

In various hands, of various sizes, the changes were rung upon these simple words:—

"MY DEAR MADAME DE FLEURY,

"I love you—I wish you were here again—I will be very very good whilst you are away. If you stay away ever so long, I shall never forget you, nor your goodness; but I hope you will soon be able to come back, and this is what I pray for every night. Sister Frances says I may tell you that I am very good, and Victoire thinks so too."

This was the substance of several of their little letters. Victoire's contained rather more information:—

"You will be glad to learn that dear Sister Frances is safe, and that the good chestnut-woman, in whose cellar she took refuge, did not get into any difficulty. After you were gone, M. T— said that he did not think it worth while to pursue her, as it was only you he wanted to humble. Manon, who has, I do not know how, means of knowing, told me this. Sister Frances is now with her abbess, who, as well as everybody else that knows her, is very fond of her. What was a convent is no longer a convent—the nuns are turned out of it. Sister Frances' health is not so good as it used to be, though she never complains. I am sure she suffers much; she has never been the same person since that day when we were driven from our happy schoolroom. It is all destroyed—the garden and everything. It is now a dismal sight. Your absence also afflicts Sister Frances much, and she is in great anxiety about all of us.

She has the six little ones with her every day in her own apartment, and goes on teaching them as she used to do. We six eldest go to see her as often as we can. I should have begun, my dear Madame de Fleury, by telling you, that, the day after you left Paris, I went to deliver all the letters you were so very kind to write for us in the midst of your hurry. Your friends have been exceedingly good to us, and have got places for us all. Rose is with Madame la Grace, your mantua-maker, who says she is more handy and more expert at cutting out than girls she has had these three years. Marianne is in the service of Madame de V—, who has lost a great part of her large fortune, and cannot afford to keep her former waiting-maid. Madame de V— is well pleased with Marianne, and bids me tell you that she thanks you for her. Indeed, Marianne, though she is only fourteen, can do everything her lady wants. Susanne is with a confectioner. She gave Sister Frances a box of bonbons of her own making this morning; and Sister Frances, who is a judge, says they are excellent—she only wishes you could taste them. Annette and I (thanks to your kindness!) are in the same service with Madame Feuillot, the brodeuse, to whom you recommended us. She is not discontented with our work, and, indeed, sent a very civil message yesterday to Sister Frances on this subject; but believe it is too flattering for me to repeat in this letter. We shall do our best to give her satisfaction. She is glad to find that we can write tolerably, and that we can make out bills and keep accounts, this being particularly convenient to her at present, as the young man she had in the shop is become an orator, and good for nothing but la chose publique; her son, who could have supplied his place, is ill; and Madame Feuillot herself, not having had, as she says, the advantage of such a good education as we have been blessed with, writes but badly, and knows nothing of arithmetic. Dear Madame de Fleury, how much, how very much we are obliged to you! We feel it every day more and more; in these times what would have become of us if we could do nothing useful? Who would, who could be burdened with us? Dear madame, we owe everything to you—and we can do nothing, not the least thing for you! My mother is still in bad health, and I fear will never recover; Babet is with her always, and Sister Frances is very good to her. My brother Maurice is now so good a workman that he earns a louis a week. He is very steady to his business, and never goes to the revolutionary meetings, though once he had a great mind to be an orator of the people, but never since the day that you explained to him that he knew nothing about equality and the rights of men, &c. How could I forget to tell you, that his master the smith, who was one of your guards, and who assisted you to escape, has returned without suspicion to his former trade? and he declares that he will never more meddle with public affairs. I gave him the money you left with me for him. He is very kind to my brother. Yesterday Maurice mended for Annette's mistress the lock of an English writing-desk, and he mended it so astonishingly well, that an English gentleman, who saw it, could not believe the work was done by a Frenchman; so my brother was sent for, to prove it, and they were forced to believe it. To-day he has more work than he can finish this twelve-month—all this we owe to you. I shall never forget the day when you promised that you would grant my brother's wish to be apprenticed to the smith, if I was not in a passion for a month; that cured me of being so passionate.

"Dear Madame de Fleury, I have written you too long a letter, and not so well as I can write when I am not in a hurry; but I wanted to tell you everything at once, because, may be, I shall not for a long time have so safe an opportunity of sending a letter to you.

"VICTOIRE."

Several months elapsed before Madame do Fleury received another letter from Victoire; it was short and evidently written in great distress of mind. It contained an account of her mother's death. She was now left at the early age of sixteen an orphan. Madame Feuillot, the brodeuse, with whom she lived, added few lines to her letter, penned with difficulty and strangely spelled, but, expressive of her being highly pleased with both the girls recommended to her by Madame de Fleury, especially Victoire, who she said was such a treasure to her, that she would not part with her on any account, and should consider her as a daughter. "I tell her not to grieve so much; for though she has lost one mother she has gained another for herself, who will always love her; and besides she is so useful, and in so many ways, with her pen and her needle, in accounts, and everything that is wanted in a family or a shop; she can never want employment or friends in the worst times, and none can be worse than these, especially for such pretty girls as she is, who have all their heads turned, and are taught to consider nothing a sin that used to be sins. Many gentlemen, who come to our shop, have found out that Victoire is very handsome, and tell her so; but she is so modest and prudent that I am not afraid for her. I could tell you, madame, a good anecdote on this subject, but my paper will not allow, and, besides, my writing is so difficult."

Above a year elapsed before Madame de Fleury received another letter from Victoire: this was in a parcel, of which an emigrant took charge; it contained a variety of little offerings from her pupils, instances of their ingenuity, their industry, and their affection; the last thing in the packet was a small purse labelled in this manner—

"Savings from our wages and earnings for her who taught us all we know."

CHAPTER XII

"Dans sa pompe elegante, admirez Chantilly,
De heros en heros, d'age en age, embelli."
—DE LILLE.

The health of the good Sister Frances, which had suffered much from the shock her mind received at the commencement of the revolution, declined so rapidly in the course of the two succeeding years, that she was obliged to leave Paris, and she retired to a little village in the neighbourhood of Chantilly. She chose this situation because here she was within a morning's walk of Madame de Fleury's country-seat. The Chateau de Fleury had not yet been seized as national property, nor had it suffered from the attacks of the mob, though it was in a perilous situation, within view of the high road to Paris. The Parisian populace had not yet extended their outrages to this distance from the city, and the poor people who lived on the estate of Fleury, attached from habit, principle, and gratitude, to their lord, were not disposed to take advantage of the disorder of the times, to injure the property of those from whom they had all their lives received favours and protection. A faithful old steward had the care of the castle and the grounds. Sister Frances was impatient to talk to him and to visit the chateau, which she had never seen; but for some days after her arrival in the village she was so much fatigued and so weak that she could not attempt so long a walk. Victoire had obtained permission from her mistress to accompany the nun for a few days to the country, as Annette undertook to do all the business of the shop during the absence of her companion. Victoire was fully as eager as Sister Frances to see the faithful steward and the Chateau de Fleury, and the morning was now fixed for their walk; but in the middle of the night they were awakened by the shouts of a mob, who had just entered the village fresh from the destruction of a neighbouring castle. The nun and Victoire listened; but in the midst of the horrid yells of joy no human voice, no intelligible word could be distinguished; they looked through a chink in the window-shutter and they saw the street below filled with a crowd of men, whose countenances were by turns illuminated by the glare of the torches which they brandished.

"Good Heavens!" whispered the nun to Victoire: "I should know the face of that man who is loading his musket—the very man whom I nursed ten years ago when he was ill with a gaol fever!"

This man, who stood in the midst of the crowd, taller by the head than the others, seemed to be the leader of the party; they were disputing whether they should proceed further, spend the remainder of the night in the village ale-house, or return to Paris. Their leader ordered spirits to be distributed to his associates, and exhorted them in a loud voice to proceed in their glorious work. Tossing his firebrand over his head he declared that he would never return to Paris till he had razed to the ground the Chateau de Fleury. At these words, Victoire, forgetful of all personal danger, ran out into the midst of the mob, pressed her way up to the leader of these ruffians, caught him by the arm, exclaiming, "You will not touch a stone in the Chateau de Fleury—I have my reasons—I say you will not suffer a stone in the Chateau de Fleury to be touched."

"And why not?" cried the man, turning astonished; "and who are you that I should listen to you?"

"No matter who I am," said Victoire; "follow me and I will show you one to whom you will not refuse to listen. Here!—here she is," continued Victoire, pointing to the nun, who had followed her in amazement; "here is one to whom you will listen—yes, look at her well: hold the light to her face."

The nun, in a supplicating attitude, stood in speechless expectation.

"Ay, I see you have gratitude, I know you will have mercy," cried Victoire, watching the workings in the countenance of the man; "you will save the Chateau de Fleury for her sake—who saved your life."

"I will," cried this astonished chief of a mob, fired with sudden generosity. "By my faith you are a brave girl, and a fine girl, and know how to speak to the heart, and in the right moment. Friends, citizens, this nun, though she is a nun, is good for something. When I lay ill with a fever, and not a soul else to help me, she came and gave me medicines and food—in short, I owe my life to her. 'Tis ten years ago, but I remember it well, and now it is our turn to rule, and she shall be paid as she deserves. Not a stone of the Chateau de Fleury shall be touched!"

With loud acclamations the mob joined in the generous enthusiasm of the moment and followed their leader peaceably out of the village. All this passed with such rapidity as scarcely to leave the impression of reality upon the mind. As soon as the sun rose in the morning Victoire looked out for the turrets of the Chateau de Fleury, and she saw that they were safe—safe in the midst of the surrounding devastation. Nothing remained of the superb palace of Chantilly but the white arches of its foundation.

CHAPTER XIII

"When thy last breath, ere Nature sank to rest
Thy meek submission to thy God expressed;
When thy last look, ere thought and feeling fled,
A mingled gleam of hope and triumph shed;
What to thy soul its glad assurance gave—
Its hope in death, its triumph o'er the grave?
The sweet remembrance of unblemished youth,

Th' inspiring voice of innocence and truth!"
—ROGERS.

The good Sister Frances, though she had scarcely recovered from the shock of the preceding night, accompanied Victoire to the Chateau de Fleury. The gates were opened for them by the old steward and his son Basile, who welcomed them with all the eagerness with which people welcome friends in time of adversity. The old man showed them the place; and through every apartment of the castle went on talking of former times, and with narrative fondness told anecdotes of his dear master and mistress. Here his lady used to sit and read—here was the table at which she wrote—this was the sofa on which she and the ladies sat the very last day she was at the castle, at the open windows of the hall, whilst all the tenants and people of the village were dancing on the green.

"Ay, those were happy times," said the old man; "but they will never return."

"Never! Oh do not say so," cried Victoire.

"Never during my life, at least," said the nun in a low voice, and with a look of resignation.

Basile, as he wiped the tears from his eyes, happened to strike his arm against the chord of Madame de Fleury's harp, and the sound echoed through the room.

"Before this year is at an end," cried Victoire, "perhaps that harp will be struck again in this Chateau by Madame de Fleury herself. Last night we could hardly have hoped to see these walls standing this morning, and yet it is safe—not a stone touched! Oh, we shall all live, I hope, to see better times!"

Sister Frances smiled, for she would not depress Victoire's enthusiastic hope: to please her, the good nun added, that she felt better this morning than she had felt for months, and Victoire was happier than she had been since Madame de Fleury left France. But, alas! it was only a transient gleam. Sister Frances relapsed and declined so rapidly, that even Victoire, whose mind was almost always disposed to hope, despaired of her recovery. With placid resignation, or rather with mild confidence, this innocent and benevolent creature met the approach of death. She seemed attached to earth only by affection for those whom she was to leave in this world. Two of the youngest of the children who had formerly been placed under her care, and who were not yet able to earn their own subsistence, she kept with her, and in the last days of her life she continued her instructions to them with the fond solicitude of a parent. Her father confessor, an excellent man, who never even in these dangerous times shrank from his duty, came to Sister Frances in her last moments, and relieved her mind from all anxiety, by promising to place the two little children with the lady who had been abbess of her convent, who would to the utmost of her power protect and provide for them suitably. Satisfied by this promise, the good Sister Frances smiled upon Victoire, who stood beside her bed, and with that smile upon her countenance expired.—It was some time before the little children seemed to comprehend, or to believe, that Sister Frances was dead: they had never before seen any one die; they had no idea what it was to die, and their first feeling was astonishment; they did not seem to understand why Victoire wept. But the next day when no Sister Frances spoke to them, when every hour they missed some accustomed kindness from her,—when presently they saw the preparations for her funeral,—when they heard that she was to be buried in the earth, and that they should never see her more,—they could neither play nor eat, but sat in a corner holding each other's hands, and watching everything that was done for the dead by Victoire.

In those times, the funeral of a nun, with a priest attending, would not have been permitted by the populace. It was therefore performed as secretly as possible: in the middle of the night the coffin was carried to the burial-place of the Fleury family; the old steward, his son Basile, Victoire, and the good father confessor, were the only persons present. It is necessary to mention this, because the facts were afterwards misrepresented.

CHAPTER XIV

"The character is lost!
Her head adorned with lappets, pinned aloft,
And ribands streaming gay, superbly raised,
Indebted to some smart wig-weaver's hand
For more than half the tresses it sustains."
—COWPER.

Upon her return to Paris, Victoire felt melancholy; but she exerted herself as much as possible in her usual occupation; finding that employment and the consciousness of doing her duty were the best remedies for sorrow.

One day as she was busy settling Madame Feuillot's accounts a servant came into the shop and inquired for Mademoiselle Victoire: he presented her a note, which she found rather difficult to decipher. It was signed by her cousin Manon, who desired to see Victoire at her hotel. "Her hotel!" repeated Victoire with astonishment. The servant assured her that one of the finest hotels in Paris belonged to his lady, and that he was commissioned to show her the way to it. Victoire found her cousin in a magnificent house, which had formerly belonged to the Prince de Salms. Manon, dressed in the disgusting, indecent extreme of the mode, was seated under a richly-fringed canopy. She burst into a loud laugh as Victoire entered.

"You look just as much astonished as I expected," cried she. "Great changes have happened since I saw you last—I always told you, Victoire, I knew the world better than you did. What has come of all your schooling, and your mighty goodness, and your gratitude truly? Your patroness is banished and a beggar, and you a drudge in the shop of a brodeuse, who makes you work your fingers to the bone, no doubt. Now you shall see the difference. Let me show you my house; you know it was formerly the hotel of the Prince de Salms, he that was guillotined the other day; but you know nothing, for you have been out of Paris this month, I understand. Then I must tell you that my friend Villeneuf has acquired an immense fortune! by assignats made in the course of a fortnight. I say an immense fortune! and has bought this fine house. Now do you begin to understand?"

"I do not clearly know whom you mean by 'your friend Villeneuf,'" said Victoire.

"The hairdresser who lived in our street," said Manon; "he became a great patriot, you know, and orator; and, what with his eloquence and his luck in dealing in assignats, he has made his fortune and mine."

"And yours! then he is your husband?"

"That does not follow—that is not necessary—but do not look so shocked—everybody goes on the sane way now; besides, I had no other resource—I must have starved—I could not earn my bread as you do. Besides, I was too delicate for hard work of any sort—and besides—but come, let me show you my house—you have no idea how fine it is."

With anxious ostentation Manon displayed all her riches to excite Victoire's envy.

"Confess, Victoire," said she at last, "that you think me the happiest person you have ever known.—You do not answer; whom did you ever know that was happier?"

"Sister Frances, who died last week, appeared to be much happier," said Victoire.

"The poor nun!" said Manon, disdainfully. "Well, and whom do you think the next happiest?"

"Madame de Fleury."

"An exile and a beggar!—Oh, you are jesting now, Victoire—or—envious. With that sanctified face, citoyenne—perhaps I should say Mademoiselle—Victoire you would be delighted to change places with me this instant. Come, you shall stay with me a week to try how you like it."

"Excuse me," said Victoire, firmly; "I cannot stay with you, Manon; you have chosen one way of life and I another—quite another. I do not repent my choice—may you never repent yours!—Farewell!"

"Bless me! what airs! and with what dignity she looks! Repent of my choice!—a likely thing, truly. Am not I at the top of the wheel?"

"And may not the wheel turn?" said Victoire.

"Perhaps it may," said Manon; "but till it does I will enjoy myself. Since you are of a different humour, return to Madame Feuillot, and figure upon cambric and muslin, and make out bills, and nurse old nuns all the days of your life. You will never persuade me, however, that you would not change places with me if you could. Stay till you are tried, Mademoiselle Victoire. Who was ever in love with you or your virtues?—Stay till you are tried."

CHAPTER XV

"But beauty, like the fair Hesperian tree,
Laden with blooming gold, had need the guard
Of dragon watch with unenchanted eye
To save her blossoms, or defend her fruit."
—MILTON.

The trial was nearer than either Manon or Victoire expected. Manon had scarcely pronounced the last words when the ci-devant hairdresser burst into the room, accompanied by several of his political associates, who met to consult measures for the good of the nation. Among these patriots was the Abbe Tracassier.

"Who is that pretty girl who is with you, Manon?" whispered he; "a friend of yours, I hope?"

Victoire left the room immediately, but not before the profligate abbe had seen enough to make him wish to see more. The next day he went to Madame Feuillot's under pretence of buying some embroidered handkerchiefs; he paid Victoire a profusion of extravagant compliments, which made no impression upon her innocent heart, and which appeared ridiculous to her plain good sense. She did not know who he was, nor did Madame Feuillot; for though she had often heard of the abbe, yet she had never seen him. Several succeeding days he returned, and addressed himself to Victoire, each time with increasing freedom. Madame Feuillot, who had the greatest confidence in her, left her entirely to her own discretion. Victoire begged her friend Annette to do the business of the shop, and stayed at work in the back parlour. Tracassier was much disappointed by her absence; but as he thought no great ceremony necessary in his proceedings, he made his name known in a haughty manner to Madame de Feuillot, and desired that he might be admitted into the back parlour, as he had something of consequence to say to Mademoiselle Victoire in private. Our readers will not require to have a detailed account of this tete-a-tete; it is sufficient to say that the disappointed and exasperated abbe left the house muttering imprecations. The next morning a note came to Victoire apparently from Manon: it was directed by her, but the inside was written by an unknown hand, and continued these words:—

"You are a charming, but incomprehensible girl—since you do not like compliments, you shall not be addressed with empty flattery. It is in the power of the person who dictates this, not only to make you as rich and great as your cousin Manon, but also to restore to fortune and to their country the friends for whom, you are most interested. Their fate as well as your own is in your power: if you send a favourable answer to this note, the persons alluded to will, to-morrow, be struck from the list of emigrants, and reinstated in their former possessions. If your answer is decidedly unfavourable, the return of your friends to France will be thenceforward impracticable, and their chateau, as well as their house in Paris, will be declared national property, and sold without delay to the highest bidder. To you, who have as much understanding as beauty, it is unnecessary to say more. Consult your heart, charming Victoire! be happy, and make others happy. This moment is decisive of your fate and of theirs, for you have to answer a man of a most decided character."

Victoire's answer was as follows:—

"My friends would not, I am sure, accept of their fortune, or consent to return to their country, upon the conditions proposed; therefore I have no merit in rejecting them."

Victoire had early acquired good principles, and that plain steady good sense, which goes straight to its object, without being dazzled or imposed upon by sophistry. She was unacquainted with the refinements of sentiment, but she distinctly knew right from wrong, and had sufficient resolution to abide by the right. Perhaps many romantic heroines might have thought it a generous self-devotion to have become in similar circumstances the mistress of Tracassier; and those who are skilled "to make the worst appear the better cause" might have made such an act of heroism the foundation of an interesting, or at least a fashionable novel. Poor Victoire had not received an education sufficiently refined to enable her to understand these mysteries of sentiment. She was even simple enough to flatter herself that this libertine patriot would not fulfil his threats, and that these had been made only with a view to terrify her into compliance. In this opinion, however, she found herself mistaken. M. Tracassier was indeed a man of the most decided character, if this form may properly be applied to those who act uniformly in consequence of their ruling passion. The Chateau de Fleury was seized as national property. Victoire heard this bad news from the old steward, who was turned out of the castle, along with his son, the very day after her rejection of the proposed conditions.

"I could not have believed that any human creature could be so wicked!" exclaimed Victoire, glowing with indignation: but indignation gave way to sorrow.

"And the Chateau de Fleury is really seized?—and you, good old man, are turned out of the place where you were born?—and you too, Basile?—and Madame de Fleury will never come back again!—and perhaps she may be put into prison in a foreign country, and may die for want—and I might have prevented all this!"

Unable to shed a tear, Victoire stood in silent consternation, whilst Annette explained to the good steward and his son the whole transaction. Basile, who was naturally of an impetuous temper, was so transported with indignation, that he would have gone instantly with the note from Tracassier to denounce him before the whole National Convention, if he had not been restrained by his more prudent father. The old steward represented to him, that as the note was neither signed nor written by the hand of Tracassier, no proof could be brought home to him, and the attempt to convict one of so powerful a party would only bring certain destruction upon the accusers. Besides, such was at this time the general depravity of manners, that numbers would keep the guilty in countenance. There was no crime which the mask of patriotism could not cover. "There is one comfort we have in our misfortunes, which these men can never have," said the old man; "when their downfall comes, and come it will most certainly, they will not feel as we do, INNOCENT. Victoire, look up! and do not give way to despair—all will yet be well."

"At all events, you have done what is right—so do not reproach yourself," said Basile. "Everybody—I mean everybody who is good for anything—must respect, admire, and love you, Victoire."

CHAPTER XVI

"Ne mal cio che v'annoja,
Quello e vero gioire
Che nasce da virtude dopo il soffrire."

Basile had not seen without emotion the various instances of goodness which Victoire showed during the illness of Sister Frances. Her conduct towards M. Tracassier increased his esteem and attachment; but he forbore to declare his affection, because he could not, consistently with prudence, or with gratitude to his father, think of marrying, now that he was not able to maintain a wife and family. The honest earnings of many years of service had been wrested from the old steward at the time the Chateau de Fleury was seized, and he now depended on the industry of his son for the daily support of his age. His dependence was just, and not likely to be disappointed; for he had given his son an education suitable to his condition in life. Basile was an exact arithmetician, could write an excellent hand, and was a ready draughtsman and surveyor. To bring these useful talents into action, and to find employment for them with men by whom they would be honestly rewarded, was the only difficulty—a difficulty which Victoire's brother Maurice soon removed. His reputation as a smith had introduced him, among his many customers, to a gentleman of worth and scientific knowledge, who was at this time employed to make models and plans of all the fortified places in Europe; he was in want of a good clerk and draughtsman, of whose integrity he could be secure. Maurice mentioned his friend Basile; and upon inquiry into his character, and upon trial of his abilities, he was found suited to the place, and was accepted. By his well-earned salary he supported himself and his father; and began, with the sanguine hopes of a young man, to flatter himself that he should soon be rich enough to marry, and that then he might declare his attachment to Victoire. Notwithstanding all his boasted prudence, he had betrayed sufficient symptoms of his passion to have rendered a declaration unnecessary to any clear-sighted observer: but Victoire was not thinking of conquests; she was wholly occupied with a scheme of earning a certain sum of money for her benefactress, who was now, as she feared, in want. All Madame de Fleury's former pupils contributed their share to the common stock; and the mantua-maker, the confectioner, the servants of different sorts, who had been educated at her school, had laid by, during the years of her banishment, an annual portion of their wages and savings: with the sum which Victoire now added to the fund, it amounted to ten thousand livres. The person who undertook to carry this money to Madame de Fleury, was Francois, her former footman, who had procured a pass to go to England as a hairdresser. The night before he set out was a happy night for Victoire, as all her companions met, by Madame Feuillot's invitation, at her house; and after tea they had the pleasure of packing up the little box, in which each, besides the money, sent some token their gratitude, and some proof of their ingenuity. They would with all their hearts have sent twice as many souvenirs as Francois could carry.

"D'abord c'est impossible!" cried he, when he saw the box that was prepared for him to carry to England: but his good nature was unable to resist the entreaties of each to have her offering carried, "which would take up no room."

He departed—arrived safe in England—found out Madame de Fleury, who was in real distress, in obscure lodgings at Richmond. He delivered the money, and all the presents of which he had taken charge: but the person to whom she entrusted a letter, in answer to Victoire, was not so punctual, or was more unlucky: for the letter never reached her, and she and her companions were long uncertain whether their little treasure had been received. They still continued, however, with indefatigable gratitude, to lay by a portion of their earnings for their benefactress; and the pleasure they had in this perseverance made them more than amends for the loss of some little amusements, and for privations to which they submitted in consequence of their resolution.

In the meantime, Basile, going on steadily with his employments, advanced every day in the favour of his master, and his salary was increased in proportion to his abilities and industry; so that he thought he could now, without any imprudence, marry. He consulted his father, who approved of his choice; he consulted Maurice as to the probability of his being accepted by Victoire; and encouraged by both his father and his friend, he was upon the eve of addressing himself to Victoire, when he was prevented by a new and unforeseen misfortune. His father was taken up, by an emissary of Tracassier's, and brought before one of their revolutionary committees, where he was accused of various acts of incivism. Among other things equally criminal, it was proved that one Sunday, when he went to see Le Petit Trianon, then a public-house, he exclaimed, "C'est ici que le canaille danse, et que les honnetes gens pleurent!"

Basile was present at this mock examination of his father—he saw him on the point of being dragged to prison—when a hint was given that he might save his father by enlisting immediately, and going with the army out of France. Victoire was full in Basile's recollection; but there was no other means of saving his father. He enlisted, and in twenty-four hours left Paris.

What appear to be the most unfortunate circumstances of life often prove ultimately the most advantageous—indeed, those who have knowledge, activity, and integrity, can convert the apparent blanks in the lottery of fortune into prizes. Basile was recommended to his commanding officer by the gentleman who had lately employed him as a clerk; his skill in drawing plans, and in taking rapid surveys of the country through which they passed, was extremely useful to his general, and his integrity made it safe to trust him as a secretary. His commanding officer, though a brave man, was illiterate, and a secretary was to him a necessary of life. Basile was not only useful, but agreeable; without any mean arts, or servile adulation, he pleased by simply showing the desire to oblige and the ability to serve.

"Diable!" exclaimed the general one day, as he looked at Basile's plan of a town which the army was besieging. "How comes it that you are able to do all these things? But you have a genius for this sort of work, apparently."

"No, sir," said Basile, "these things were taught to me when I was a child by a good friend."

"A good friend he was, indeed! he did more for you than if he had given you a fortune; for, in these times, that might have been soon taken from you; but now you have the means of making a fortune for yourself."

This observation of the general's, obvious as it may seem, is deserving of the serious consideration of those who have children of their own to educate, or who have the disposal of money for public charities. In these times no sensible person will venture to pronounce that a change of fortune and station may not await the highest and the lowest; whether we rise or fall in the scale of society, personal qualities and knowledge will be valuable. Those who fall cannot be destitute, and those who rise cannot be ridiculous or contemptible, if they have been prepared for their fortune by proper education. In shipwreck those who carry their all in their minds are the most secure.

But to return to Basile. He had sense enough not to make his general jealous of him by any unseasonable display of his talents, or any officious intrusion of advice, even upon subjects which he best understood.

The talents of the warrior and the secretary were in such different lines, that there was no danger of competition; and the general, finding in his secretary the soul of all the arts, good sense, gradually acquired the habit of asking his opinion on every subject that came within his department. It happened that the general received orders from the Directory at Paris to take a certain town, let it cost what it would, within a given time: in his perplexity he exclaimed before Basile against the unreasonableness of these orders, and declared his belief that it was impossible he should succeed, and that this was only a scheme of his enemies to prepare his ruin. Basile had attended to the operations of the engineer who acted under the general, and perfectly recollected the model of the mines of this town, which he had seen when he was employed as draughtsman by his Parisian friend. He remembered that there was formerly an old mine that had been stopped up somewhere near the place where the engineer was at work; he mentioned in private his suspicions to the general, who gave orders in consequence. The old mine was discovered, cleared out, and by these means the town was taken the day before the time appointed. Basile did not arrogate to himself any of the glory of this success; he kept his general's secret and his confidence. Upon their return to Paris, after a fortunate campaign, the general was more grateful than some others have been, perhaps because more room was given by Basile's prudence for the exercise of this virtue.

"My friend," said he to Basile, "you have done me a great service by your counsel, and a greater still by holding your tongue. Speak now, and tell me freely if there is anything I can do for you. You see, as a victorious general, I have the upper hand amongst these fellows—Tracassier's scheme to ruin me missed—whatever I ask will at this moment be granted; speak freely, therefore."

Basile asked what he knew Victoire most desired—that Monsieur and Madame de Fleury should be struck from the list of emigrants, and that their property now in the hands of the nation should be restored to them. The general promised that this should be done. A warm contest ensued upon the subject between him and Tracassier, but the general stood firm; and Tracassier, enraged, forgot his usual cunning, and quarrelling irrevocably with a party now more powerful than his own, he and his adherents were driven from that station in which they had so long tyrannised. From being the rulers of France, they in a few hours became banished men, or, in the phrase of the times, des deportes.

We must not omit to mention the wretched end of Manon. The man with whom she lived perished by the guillotine. From his splendid house she went upon the stage, did not succeed, sank from one degree of profligacy to another, and at last died in an hospital.

In the meantime, the order for the restoration of the Fleury property, and for permission for the Fleury family to return to France, was made out in due form, and Maurice begged to be the messenger of these good tidings—he set out for England with the order.

Victoire immediately went down to the Chateau de Fleury, to get everything in readiness for the reception of the family.

Exiles are expeditious in their return to their native country. Victoire had but just time to complete her preparations, when Monsieur and Madame de Fleury arrived at Calais. Victoire had assembled all her companions, all Madame de Fleury's former pupils; and the hour when she was expected home, they, with the peasants of the neighbourhood, were all in their holiday clothes, and, according to the custom of the country, singing and dancing. Without music and dancing there is no perfect joy in France. Never was fete du village or fete du Seigneur more joyful than this.

The old steward opened the gate, the carriage drove in. Madame de Fleury saw that home which she had little expected evermore to behold, but all other thoughts were lost in the pleasure of meeting her beloved pupils.

"My children!" cried she, as they crowded round her the moment she got out of her carriage—"my dear, good children!"

It was all she could say. She leaned on Victoire's arm as she went into the house, and by degrees recovering from the almost painful excess of pleasure, began to enjoy what she yet only confusedly felt.

Several of her pupils were so much grown and altered in their external appearance, that she could scarcely recollect them till they spoke, and then their voices and the expression of their countenances brought their childhood fully to her memory. Victoire, she thought, was changed the least, and at this she rejoiced.

The feeling and intelligent reader will imagine all the pleasure that Madame de Fleury enjoyed this day; nor was it merely the pleasure of a day. She heard from all her friends, with prolonged satisfaction, repeated accounts of the good conduct of these young people during her absence. She learned with delight how her restoration to her country and her fortune had been effected; and is it necessary to add, that Victoire consented to marry Basile, and that she was suitably portioned, and, what is better still, that she was perfectly happy? Monsieur de Fleury rewarded the attachment and good conduct of Maurice by taking him into his service, and making him his manager under the old steward at the Chateau de Fleury.

On Victoire's wedding-day Madame de Fleury produced all the little offerings of gratitude which she had received from her and her companions during her exile. It was now her turn to confer favours, and she knew how to confer them both with grace and judgment.

"No gratitude in human nature! No gratitude in the lower classes of the people!" cried she; "how much those are mistaken who think so! I wish they could know my history, and the history of these my children, and they would acknowledge their error."

Maria Edgeworth – A Short Biography

Maria Edgeworth was born at Black Bourton, Oxfordshire on January 1st 1768, the second child of Richard Lovell Edgeworth and Anna Maria Edgeworth (née Elers).

Her early years were with her mother's family in England. Sadly, her mother died when Maria was only five. When her father married his second wife, Honora Sneyd, in 1773, the family went to live at his estate, Edgeworthstown, in County Longford, Ireland.

Maria was later sent to Mrs. Lattafière's school in Derby after Honora fell ill in 1775. There she studied dancing, French and other subjects. After Honora died in 1780 Maria's father married Honora's sister, Elizabeth, causing much social disapproved.

Maria transferred to Mrs. Devis's school in Upper Wimpole Street, London. Her father began to focus more attention on Maria in 1781 when she nearly lost her sight to an eye infection.

She returned home to Ireland at 14, and took charge of her younger siblings. She herself was home-tutored by her father in Irish economics and politics, science, literature and law. Despite her youth literature was in her blood.

She became her father's assistant in managing the Edgeworthstown estate, which had become run-down during the family's absence. Maria would now live and write there for the rest of her life.

With her father she began a lifelong academic collaboration. She meticulously detailed daily Irish life; a valuable lodestone of references for later use in her novels. Maria mixed with the Anglo-Irish gentry, and her aunt, Margaret Ruxton of Blackcastle, supplied her with the novels of Anne Radcliffe and William Godwin and encouraged her ambition to write.

Edgeworth's first published work in 1795 was 'Letters for Literary Ladies'. That same year 'An Essay on the Noble Science of Self-Justification', written for a female audience, states that the fair sex is endowed with an art of self-justification and women should use their gifts to continually challenge the force and power of men, especially their husbands, with wit and intelligence.

In 1796 her first children's book, 'The Parent's Assistant', which included the much loved short story 'The Purple Jar' was published.

In 1798 her father married for the fourth and last time, this time to Frances Beaufort. Frances was a year younger than Maria and they quickly became close.

'Practical Education' (1798) is a progressive work on education that combines the ideas of Locke and Rousseau with scientific inquiry. Edgeworth believed that "learning should be a positive experience and that the discipline of education is more important during the formative years than the acquisition of knowledge." The ultimate goal of Edgeworth's system was to create an independent thinker who understands the consequences of his or her actions.

Her first novel, 'Castle Rackrent' (1800) was published anonymously without her father's knowledge. It was an immediate success and firmly established Maria's appeal to the public.

'Belinda' (1801), was her first full-length novel. It dealt with love, courtship, and marriage, and she examined these as conflicts within her "own personality and environment; conflicts between reason and feeling, restraint and individual freedom, and society and free spirit." Startlingly, 'Belinda' also included a depiction of interracial marriage between an African servant and an English farm-girl. Later editions of the novel, in line with unforgiving times, removed these sections.

Frances also pushed the family to travel more first London (1800), the Midlands (1802) and later the continent; first to Brussels and then to France. They met all the notables, with Maria even receiving a proposal of marriage from a Swedish courtier.

'Tales of Fashionable Life' (1809 and 1812) is a 2-series collection of short stories that often had its focus on the life of women. The second series was so successful that she was now the most commercially successful novelist of her age and ranked alongside her contemporaries Jane Austen and Sir Walter Scott.

On a visit to London in 1813, she met many notables including Lord Byron. She entered into a long correspondence with Sir Walter Scott after the publication of 'Waverley' in 1814, in which he acknowledged her influence, and they formed a lasting friendship. She visited him in Scotland at Abbotsford House in 1823 and the following year he visited Edgeworthstown.

After debating the issue with the economist David Ricardo, Maria came to believe that better management and the further use of science in agriculture would raise food production and help to lower prices. They were both in favour of Catholic Emancipation, enfranchisement for Catholics without property restrictions, agricultural reform and increased educational opportunities for women.

She worked particularly hard to improve the living standards of the poor in Edgeworthstown and to provide schools for the local children whatever their denomination.

After her father's death in 1817 she edited his memoirs, and extended them with her biographical addenda. Her father had married 4 times and sired 22 children. At the height of her creative endeavours, Maria had written, "Seriously it was to please my Father I first exerted myself to write, to please him I continued."

Maria worked for the relief of the famine-stricken Irish peasants during the Irish Potato Famine. She wrote 'Orlandino' and gave the proceeds to the Relieve Fund. However, during the famine her 'business head' insisted that only those tenants who had paid their full rent would receive any relief. She also punished any tenants who voted against her Tory preferences.

'Helen' (1834) is Maria Edgeworth's final novel, the only one she wrote after her father's death. Here the focus was on characters and situation and not moral lessons.

William Rowan Hamilton was elected president of the Royal Irish Academy and Maria's advice was constantly sought especially regarding literature in Ireland. She suggested that women should be allowed to participate in Academy events. Hamilton made Maria an honorary member in 1837.

After a visit to see her relations Maria was struck with severe chest pains and died suddenly of a heart attack in Edgeworthstown on 22nd May 1849. She was 81.

Maria Edgeworth is buried in the family tomb at St. John's Church, Edgeworthstown, Longford, Ireland.

Maria Edgeworth – A Concise Bibliography

Letters for Literary Ladies (1795) Second Edition (1798)
An Essay on the Noble Science of Self-Justification (1795)
The Parent's Assistant (1796)
Practical Education (1798) (2 Vols; collaborated with her father and step-mother)
Castle Rackrent (1800) Novel
Early Lessons (1801)
Moral Tales (1801)
Belinda (1801) Novel
The Mental Thermometer (1801)
Essay on Irish Bulls (1802)
Popular Tales (1804)
The Modern Griselda (1804)
Moral Tales for Young People (1805) (6 Vols)
Leonora (1806)
Essays in Professional Education (1809)
Tales of Fashionable Life (1809)
Ennui (1809) Novel
The Absentee (1812) Novel
Patronage (1814) Novel
Harrington (1817) Novel
Ormond (1817) Novel
Comic Dramas (1817)
Memoirs of Richard Lovell Edgeworth (1820) Editor
Rosamond: A Sequel to Early Lessons (1821)

Frank: A Sequel to Frank in Early Lessons (1822)
Tomorrow (1823) Novel
Helen (1834) novel
Orlandino (1848) Temperance novel

www.ingramcontent.com/pod-product-compliance
Lightning Source LLC
Chambersburg PA
CBHW021936170626
46807CB00007B/3136